First published in Great Britain in 1999 by Fusion Press, a division of Satin Publications Limited.

This book is copyright under the Berne Convention. All rights reserved. No part of this publication may be reproduced, stored in a retrieval system, or transmitted in any form or by any means, electronic, mechanical, photocopying, recording or otherwise, without prior written permission of the publisher.

Fusion Press
a division of
Satin Publications Limited
20 Queen Anne Street
London W1M 0AY
Email: sheenadewan@compuserve.com

Cover: ©1999 Nickolai Globe
Layout: Justine Hounam
Printed and bound by The Bath Press Ltd.

©1999 Andy Gravette
ISBN: 1-901250-39-3

Classic Cuban Cookery

Andy Gravette

About the Author

Andy Gravette was born in Windsor, England and spent his formative years in West Sussex. From a background as a foreign correspondent on the Sunday Times of London, reporting from Africa and the Middle East, the author edited several magazines before writing his first book. He made several tours of the Caribbean and first visited Cuba in 1984. Since then, Andy has written almost 30 books, including seven published works on Cuba. As a lecturer, he now accompanies specialist tours of Cuba, giving talks on the natural history, culture, history, tobacco, rum and food of the island. He now lives just outside of London with his wife, Louisa, a former actress.

Contents

Weights and Measures 1

Introduction 3

Starters 9

Snacks 17

Salads 29

Soups 39

Meat Dishes 53

Sauces 85

Seafood Dishes 105

Fish Dishes 119

Vegetarian and Vegetable Dishes 135

Desserts 159

Coffees 187

Cocktails 195

Appendix 213

Alternative Ingredients 217

Index 221

Weights and Measures

Conversions into Imperial and Metric Measurements

Although many cooks still use the British Imperial weights (Avoirdupois) and measures, metric is fast becoming the accepted method in the kitchen. Imperial does not concert easily into metric, and most recipes will round the figures either up or down. Classic Cuban Cookery gives accuracy to the nearest 10 g in the recipes.

Solid weights

Imperial	Metric Recommended
1 ounce	25 grams
2 ounces	50 grams
4 ounces	100 grams
8 ounces (1/2 pound)	225 grams
12 ounces	350 grams
14 ounces	400 grams
16 ounces (1 pound)	450 grams
2 pounds 3 ounces	1000 grams (1 kilogram)

Liquid Measures

Imperial	Metric Recommended
1/4 pint	150 millilitres
1/2 pint	275 millilitres
1 pint	570 millilitres
1 1/2 pints	900 millilitres
1 3/4 pints	1000 millilites (1 litre)

Standard spoon measures are used throughout, and spoonfulls are level measures except where specified.

1 tablespoon = 15 ml spoon
1 teaspoon = 5 ml spoon

Cup measures

These vary with the ingredient, although a general rule for the size of cup is one that contains 8 liquid ounces, 1/2 pint or 300 ml of liquid.

1 cup flour = 4 ounces (110 grams)
1 cup uncooked rice = 6 ounces (150 grams)
1 cup of sugar = 8 ounces (200 grams)

Oven temperatures

Both moderate and hot ovens are suggested in the following recipes and a moderately hot oven should be between 160-180°C and a hot oven should be between 220-230°C.

Unless otherwise stated, recipes are intended to serve 4 people.

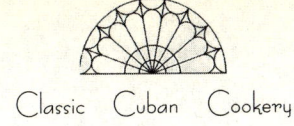

Classic Cuban Cookery

Introduction

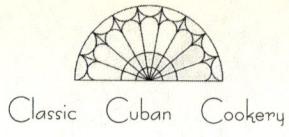

Classic Cuban Cookery

Cuban Cuisine

Typical Cuban, or creole-style cookery ('Cocina Criolla') cannot really be described as either Caribbean, African, or Latin American. Cuban cookery has emerged out of a combination of Spanish, African and tropical American tastes. Within Cuba, 'criollo' food varies from region to region, generally becoming spicier and more chilli-hot the further south one travels.

The country has an ideal climate and a rich soil perfect for the cultivation of all types of tropical and sub-tropical fruit and vegetables, as well as those from more northerly climes. Surrounded by three seas teeming with a glorious variety of fish and crustaceans, large areas of the land are set aside for cattle ranching, pig and chicken farming and hunting reserves. Acres of fruit orchard contrast with the great sea of sugar cane, which is the island's mainstay crop and huge areas are devoted to market garden crops. Almost all food in Cuba is fresh, straight from the field, garden, orchard or sea, with no artificial additives such as those found in most western countries.

Remember that some Cuban dishes can be quite spicy or hot. These creole-style dishes, suitably pepped up with the addition of a paste made from the red chilli, or 'ají'. Cuba produces a variety of chillies, from the mild Ancho, to the world-renown, fiery-hot Habanero chilli. The more African the palate, the more spicy-hot the food. Onions and garlic are liberally added to most Cuban savoury dishes, and spices add subtleties to the more exotic cuisine.

From shark, turtle or crocodile-tail steaks, to giant lobsters, succulent shrimp, and palomilla cuts from the unique Cuban strain of cattle, the menus of the island's 100 best-known restaurants occasionally reveal a gourmet's delight and some unusual culinary surprises. Vegetarians are well-catered for in Cuba, such is the wide variety of produce - from greens and root vegetables, to exotic fruits and nuts. Those with a sweet tooth will be pleased to find that sugar is the island's main crop, and Cuban ice cream is revered world-wide.

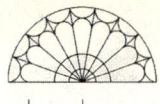

Introduction

Since the Cuban Revolution of 1959, all the island's restaurants and hotels were nationalised, and are now run under the auspices of government-controlled management companies, which are now self-funding. This provides for relatively recent competition between restaurants and hotel diners, vastly improving the culinary standards, which had declined somewhat during the 1970s and '80s. Today, investment in the tourism industry has resulted in raising the culinary excellence across the country, and the major vacation centres now offer a vast range of international as well as Cuban cuisine.

Apart from the newer tourist hotels, the country's restaurants range from converted, ancient colonial villas, historic forts and castles, rustic country ranches, early sugar baron's mansions, and legendary hotels and nightclubs dating from pre-revolutionary days. Havana, Cuba's capital city, has no less than 50 restaurants, a dozen of which have outstanding historic backgrounds, or a fascinating past. All of which serve a fine selection of classic Cuban fare.

Since 1995, many Habaneros, or people of Havana, have opened their private homes to visitors, inviting them to dine in their own parlours, in a typically Cuban atmosphere. These open houses are known as 'casas particulares', or 'paladares', literally 'palates'. Paladares generally provide traditional Cuban food, and this can range from lobster or chicken, to rice and beans, or roast pork. Many paladares are reviving the early classic Cuban recipes, some of which were largely forgotten between the 1960s and 1980s.

The potential of Cuban cuisine is practically limitless wherever the ingredients are available, and the entire country was scoured to put together this exhaustive selection of typical Cuban recipes, and details of their ingredients. The resulting compilation is the fruit of fifteen years of research - "Buen provecho!" - "Enjoy!"

Andy Gravette, 1999

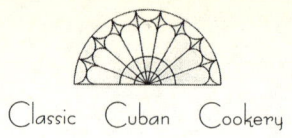

Classic Cuban Cookery

A Background to Cuban Cuisine

'Cocina Cubana', or Cuban kitchen cookery, developed over many centuries. Its early origins go back to the island's first inhabitants, the Arawak and Taino Amerindians, who migrated to Cuba from the jungles of South America. They brought with them a wealth of rare tropical plants, and numerous cooking skills. They both made bread and stews, they invented the barbecue, discovered how to preserve meats, they were excellent gardeners, and developed extraordinary methods of trapping game, and catching fish, in another of their inventions, the canoe.

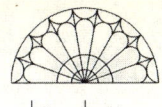

Introduction

Almost four thousand years after the Amerindians first set foot on Cuba, explorer Christopher Columbus arrived on the island in 1492. With him, and the succession of Spanish colonists, European foods and cookery methods were introduced. The Cuban climate and soil was found to be excellent for raising many Mediterranean culinary ingredients, and these combined well with the New World fruits, vegetables and spices, cultivated by the island's original inhabitants.

One hundred years after Columbus' first visit to Cuba, sugar cane became the island's leading crop. The Spanish colonists imported African slave labour to tend and process the cane. With the Africans, came a host of West African plants, and a variety of tastes and cooking methods new to the Spanish. During the height of the Spanish Main, buccaneers and pirates of various nationalities, settled in remote parts of Cuba, preying on passing shipping, and bringing with them their homeland cuisine.

During an eleven month occupation of Cuba in 1762, the English wasted no time in converting Cubans to their cookery styles and preferences, several of which can still be experienced on the island today. Also, with Captain Bligh, in the late 18th century, a variety of Pacific Ocean ingredients arrived in the Caribbean, adding several more ingredients to the Cuban kitchen table.

In 1791, three hundred years after Columbus, a slave uprising in nearby French Haiti, drove thousands of French planters and their followers to seek refuge in Cuba. These migrants brought new cookery ideas with them, and the slaves which accompanied the exiles, originating from a different part of Africa to those already in Cuba, also introduced their particular cuisine to add to the island's rich culinary mixture.

From the mid-19th century, numerous migrants arrived from the Spanish Canary Islands, again bringing with them their island cuisine to the Cuban kitchen. Emancipation came late to Cuba. After freeing their slaves, in 1880, Cuban landowners and planters, began importing large numbers of Chinese labourers to replace the African workforce. From China, came the Cuban's staple diet, rice, and a variety of Far Eastern spices and herbs previously unknown on the island.

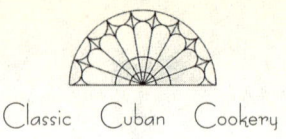

Classic Cuban Cookery

The melting pot of Cuban cookery was still not complete. The Cuban kitchen had already assimilated the culinary ingredients of Amerindian, Spanish, African, English, French, and Chinese cookery methods, including those of the Pacific Ocean, the Canary Islands, and those of the itinerant buccaneers of multifarious origins. It was during the 1920s that yet another ingredient was added to the Cuban cooking pot. Americans discovered Cuba as an offshore pleasure resort for the following forty years, and many migrated to the island to set up business, introducing the tastes and cooking methods of the United States to complete the mixture.

Thus Cuban cookery developed from origins in four continents, evolving a distinctly unique blend of tastes and culinary specialities. Since 1959, economic privations have prevented Cuban farmers from obtaining many chemical fertilisers and pest controls. This has resulted in crops being raised entirely organically. The naturally produced ingredients of Cuban cookery, plus the variety of culinary produce, and the balance of the traditional Cuban diet, produced one of the healthiest cuisines in the world.

Many of Cuba's tropical ingredients might be new to the cook from temperate climes, but those ingredients that may seem familiar often have interesting uses in Cuban cookery, as well as interesting tales about their origin.

On a visit to Cuba, not only is there a chance to sample the country's special dishes and drinks, but there is the opportunity to dine in restaurants that were once the haunt of the rich and famous during the 1940s and '50s. There are many historic sites of Havana and its surrounds to see, including traditional rum and coffee centres. There is also the time to follow in the footsteps of Ernest Hemingway and Graham Greene, and enjoy the exotic shows whilst dining in Cuba's many nightclubs, which have made its music and dance famous throughout the world. Each chapter of Classic Cuban Cookery introduced one of Havana City's historic and renowned restaurants.

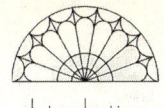

Introduction

Havana

"Enigmatic and mysteriously nostalgic, set in the scented tropics on the edge of an azure ocean, the name Havana invokes the whiff of a Cuban cigar, the mellow tang of aged rum, the bite of piquante sauce, the sounds of tango and salsa, and the velvet touch of the Caribbean sea breeze."

Most new arrivals to Havana get their first view of Cuba's bustling capital during the short drive from the airport to one of Havana's many hotels. To the first-time visitor, the monuments, and modern buildings of the Plaza de la Revolution park might seem reminiscent of many other Latin American cities. It is only when exploring its intimate corners, broad boulevards, fine promenade and old quarter, that the visitor begins to appreciate the complexity of this ancient city and the surprises that Havana has to offer. Its turbulent history summons up images of gallant Independence fighters, revolutionary heroes and celebrated literary masters. Magnificent monuments of great generals and Independence leaders like Marti, Maceo, Gomez and Garcia testify to the Cuban commitment in the struggle for freedom, as do the pictures of Che Guevara and Fidel Castro on T-shirts, placards and posters.

Wandering around Old Havana, one can hear the echoes of Ernest Hemingway and Graham Greene, who both fell in love with this city. Colonial splendour vies with neo-classical monuments and soaring skyscraper blocks rub shoulders with grand palaces. Havana is like no other city anywhere in the world and combines the Colonial historic heritage of the Old World with privileges and attributes of the New.

La Rampa mainstreet has the exuberance of Barcelona's La Rambla; El Capitoli, is a perfect replica of Washington's Capitol, and the Paseo de Marti a masterful copy of that in Madrid. The long Malecon promenade is reminiscent of the Corniche in Alexandria, or the Caracciolo in Naples, even down to the ancient fortresses dominating the seafront. The futuristic trompe d'oeil tower of the Marti monument might have come from Mexico City, La Tropicana Club is straight out of Rio de Janeiro, and the Garcia Lorca theatre

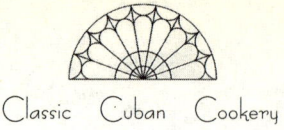

Classic Cuban Cookery

would not look out of place in the Avenue de l'Opera in Paris, or in Rome's Campidoglio Quarter. The art collection of Havana's National Museum rivals those of most European capitals, and its colonial palaces are as richly decorated as any in Granada or Seville. There is no doubt that Havana stands alone as a city of unique character and seductive attractions, all enhanced by the reflected light off the waters of the 'Blue Stream'. Once the Hub of the New World, Havana deserves a few days of any visitor's time, to explore its history, enjoy its walks and sites, eat in world-famous restaurants and revel in its famed entertainment and nightlife.

Classic Cuban Cookery

Starters

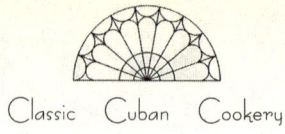

Classic Cuban Cookery

El Patio Restaurant, Havana

In the 16th century, the plot of land on which El Patio now stands belonged to Gonzalo Perez de Angulo, but it was not built on until 1760, and some of the original structure remains to this day. The Patio restaurant is so called because unlike most 18th century Spanish mansions, this 1775 villa has no carriage entrance and its doorways lead directly into the open patio courtyard.

Arched cloisters surround the cooling central fountain and a profusion of greenery shades the graceful architecture. The turtles in the fountain, singing birds and colourful butterflies make for a tropical oasis in the middle of the hectic capital. In the evenings a serenading trio sets off the relaxed atmosphere with a mixture of song and early Cuban ballads.

El Patio was restored in 1963 and the famous Cuban artist, Posada had his studio in the attic, creating many a masterpiece under El Patio's roofs. There are three dining rooms, with one on the ground floor and another on the mezzanine, and two kitchens. The top floor has a bar, La Capilla, and, around the courtyard there are two private dining rooms and a cafeteria service. Also off the patio is the mahogany-countered El Patio Bar.

Starters

Cuban starters vary considerably, from the very basic dish of diced cold vegetables, or rustically presented tapas style dishes served in coconut shells, a gourd or on banana leaves. Tapas, green tomatoes in olive oil, slices of local chorizo sausages, olives, fried plantain or cod fritters dipped in lime juice are all popular starters. Deep fried pork rind, or chicharrónes, are a favourite, as are fajitas, a word meaning 'small thin belts', because the narrow strips of marinaded, tough skirt steaks, resemble belts.

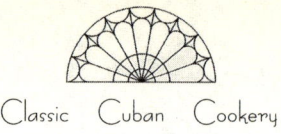

Classic Cuban Cookery

Boniato

This tuber is a form of sweet potato crossed with the jucca and cassava, which the Arawak Amerindians ate along with a variety of root crops as their staple diet. Boniato is an old Latin American word for edible, and the vegetable has a sweet white flesh. This variety of sweet potato has a chestnutty flavour and is generally boiled and mashed. Boniato should be peeled before cooking and diced and simmered for 30 to 40 minutes until they are soft.

BONIATILLO CHANGO – CHANGO-STYLE SWEET POTATOES

    450g (1lb) sweet potatoes, peeled and sliced
    350g (12oz) soft brown sugar
    3 eggs, beaten
    1 tsp lime juice
    1 tsp grated lime rind
    3 tbs Gold rum
    1/4 tsp allspice
    110ml (4 fl oz) water

Simmer potatoes in water for around 30 minutes until soft. Drain potatoes and purée. Simmer sugar, allspice, lime peel and lime juice in the water for 15 minutes and discard peel. Mash the liquid into the potatoes over a low heat, and then beat eggs into the mixture, simmering and stirring for about 3 minutes. Remove from heat and stir in the rum. Chill before serving.

Starters

Queso Fruta Bomba – Cuban Papaya Cheese

    Flesh of half a ripe papaya, peeled and deseeded
    juice of 4 oranges
    juice of 1 lime
    175g (6oz) sugar

Simmer papaya flesh in orange and lime juice until soft. Blend the soft flesh mixture and add sugar. Bring the mixture to the boil and cook until thick. Turn 'cheese' out into pre-greased dishes to serve. Serve hot or cold with bread or dry biscuits.

TAPAS

Camarones – Shrimp Tapas

    110g (4oz) peeled shrimp
    10g (1/2oz) garlic butter
    1 tsp lime juice
    55ml (2 fl oz) corn oil
    1/4 tsp chopped parsley

Heat oil in a frying pan and cook the shrimp on both sides. Add garlic butter and reduce liquid to half the original volume. Remove from heat and add lime juice. Serve hot with the juices and chopped parsley garnish.

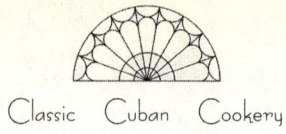

Classic Cuban Cookery

Calamares – Squid Tapas

150g (5oz) cleaned squid tubes
110ml (4 fl oz) olive oil
50g (2oz) garlic mayonnaise
1/4 tsp chopped parsley
2 tbs seasoned flour

Flour the squid rings and discard excess flour. Deep fry rings until golden. Dry rings on kitchen paper and serve with mayonnaise and parsley.

Boniato – Sweet Potato Tapas

225g (8oz) sweet potato, cut into strips
25g (1oz) cumin seeds
275ml (1/2 pint) corn oil

Deep fry sweet potatoes until golden and remove excess oil. Toss potato strips in cumin seeds until covered. Serve immediately.

Starters

Cashew

The cashew ('Anacardium occidentale') is a native of the Americas and gets his name from the local Amerindian word 'acaju'. The expensive cashew nut is one of nature's curiosities, as it is the only nut to grow outside its pod case, a red-yellow 'apple', which can itself be eaten. This cashew apple has a slightly sour taste, and so is mostly used in jams and preserves. The apple is rich in vitamins A and C and has a high phosphorus content. Known as Maranon in Cuba the evergreen tree grows up to seven metres high and is a relative of the poison ivy plant. The poisonous oil of the cashew shell is removed by sun-drying the nut before the inner shell is discarded. The nut itself can be eaten raw, but is normally roasted and served as a snack. The cashew nut contains 45 per cent fat, and 20 per cent protein. The cashew fruit contains 46 calories per 100 grams, and, because it is acrid in flavour, is more often used in jams, jellies and preserves.

CICHARRONES – PORK RIND SNACKS

    450g (1lb) pork rind, trimmed of fat
    55ml (2 fl oz) corn oil
    2 tsp salt

Cover the rind with water, and soak for 1 hour. Boil rind in water for 10 minutes. Cut rind into small pieces. Sprinkle rind with salt. Fry the rind in the oil for 15 minutes, in covered pan. Remove the cover slightly, and fry until rind is crisp and brown. Drain chicharrónes on paper towel.

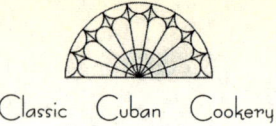

Classic Cuban Cookery

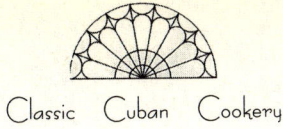
Classic Cuban Cookery

Snacks

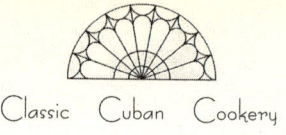

Classic Cuban Cookery

The Ambos Mundos Hotel Restaurant, Havana

The Ambos Mundos 'Both Worlds' Hotels at 153 Obispo Street on the corner of Mercaderes Street was where, in 1939, Ernest Hemingway began writing 'For Whom the Bell Tolls' and 'To Have and Have Not'. He stayed in room 511, which has been preserved as it was when the writer stayed there periodically between 1932 and 1940. For a small charge, visitors can view Hemingway's room, complete with his typewriter, a model of his boat, the Pilar, and an empty Chivas Regal whiskey bottle. The building was once an 18th century marquis' mansion, before it was converted into a hotel in the 19th century. Ernest Hemingway lived in Cuba for a total of 22 years. His books, 'Islands in the Stream' and 'The Old Man and the Sea' are about life in Cuba, and the latter won him the 1954 Nobel Prize for Literature. The writer lived in Cuba from the 1930s to 1950s and had a home, Finca Vigía, just outside Havana. He often stayed at the Ambos Mundos Hotel in Old Havana. The restaurant in this historical hotel has been restored to reflect the ambience of Hemingway's days.

Snacks

Snacks

Cuban snacks, or 'bocaditos', are often small meals in themselves. There are a number of local snack bars called 'Pío Pío', serving takeaway chicken pieces, and a government owned chain known as Quac Quac, which offers fried duck. However, the most popular snack in Cuba is pizza, albeit a more simplified version of the Italian classic - normally the pizza base is just topped with a smear of tomato paste. The ubiquitous Cuban sandwich, or bocadillo, is more often than not filled with either processed cheese or ham. Many restaurants serve pizzas in their more conventional form, but the traditional Cuban snacks are more inventive and appetising. Chicken wings in a spicy sauce are a favourite, but quite often a snack is a 'ración' (small helping) of a main meal, often in the form of a thick stew or hotpot. Tortillas, spanish omelettes or pancakes are also served as snacks, as are tamales, which are corn tortillas filled with spicy meat. Often, hotel poolsides will have a 'parrillada', or grill, where a range of hot snacks are cooked.

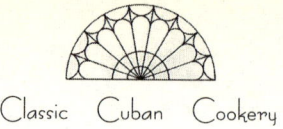

Classic Cuban Cookery

Maize

Early trading routes between Cuba and Yucatan, which is the nearest peninsula of Central America, introduced the island's inhabitants to many of the culinary delights of the Aztec and Mayan peoples, including maize. An entire religious cult had grown up around the maize plant, which had been cultivated from local grasses around 3000BC. Today, Indian Corn, known in ancient Cuba as 'mahis' or 'elote' is one of the most prolific of American vegetables, in the form of cornflakes or popcorn.
The native Arawaks of Cuba, supplemented their diet with maize, or Indian Corn. Maize, (Zea mays), Indian Corn, or Maíz, grows as a tall, single stem, up to six foot in height, with cobs of yellow or beige grains, sprouting directly from the stalk. It is planted from seed and takes 3 to 5 months to mature. The male flowers consist of feathery stalks at the top of the stem, and the female flowers are formed on the cob, lower down the stem. Tassels from the female flower entrap the pollen wafted from the male flowers, which pollinates them. Broad, flat and hard grains of maize grow in rows on the cob of the female flowers. The cob is surrounded by sheath-like leaves, which protect the grains, clinging to the central cob. The grains are eaten either raw, cooked or are ground to make bread or cereals. Corn kernels are high in sugar, which begins to convert into starch once the cob is picked. The cob itself is used as pig or cattle fodder. Maize flour is a substitute for wheat flour in Cuba, and is also eaten as a vegetable, often replacing rice or potatoes. Maize is now widely grown in Cuba, and forms the basis of many local dishes.
There are three main varieties of maize. Sweet corn is the most widely used, and is often known as Green corn, because the cob is picked before it is ripe. Sweet corn is eaten raw, boiled, or roasted, and contains 129 calories per 100 grams. Dent corn is the source of cornflour, and popcorn is so called as the kernels explode when heated, caused by the sudden expansion of water in the seed.

Snacks

Tamales Picado – Ground Beef Tamale Snacks

450g (1lb) ground beef (picado)
6 fresh cobs maize, cleaned and prepared
whole husks of 30 maize cobs
1 large onion, finely chopped
6 cloves garlic, finely chopped
2 Jalapeno chillies, seeded and finely chopped
1 green sweet bell pepper, seeded and finely chopped
80ml (1/4 cup) butter
250ml (9 fl oz) maize oil
1 tsp white wine vinegar
2 tsp olive oil
2 spring onions, finely chopped
1/2 tsp mixed herbs
1 tsp fresh oregano, chopped fine
2 gherkins, chopped fine
6 olives, chopped fine
1 tsp capers
2 hard boiled eggs, chopped small
2 tbs tomato purée
1/2 tsp each of salt and black ground pepper
sprig fresh coriander
1 bay leaf
1 tsp cumin seed

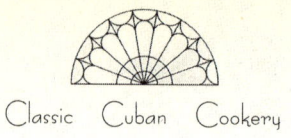

Classic Cuban Cookery

Cut thin strips out of 8 husks, for tying the tamales. Mash the garlic, oregano, half the salt and pepper to a paste. Mix the mash into the meat with olive oil and vinegar. Fry onion, chillies and bell pepper for about 10 minutes. Add meat mix and brown for about 10 minutes, stirring. Add mixed herbs, capers, gherkins, olives, and tomato purée. Add the eggs, stirring occasionally. Season with rest of salt and pepper, and cook for 4 minutes. Grate the maize cob kernels finely, into a basin. Mix the fried mixture into the grated maize.

Place 3 corn husks flat, overlapping the two centre edges. Arrange them to form a pointed tube. Fold the pointed end of the tube up, to close it at one end. Spoon mixture into top of tube, holding the tube together. Press mixture down into the tube with the back of a spoon. Take three more husks to close the top. Place these, pointed ends up, around the filled tube. The husks' pointed ends should stand proud of the filled tube. Hold the filled tube enclosed by the husks, upright. Fold the projecting pointed end in, to seal the top. Take a long strip of husk, and tie around tamale 'waist'. Take another long strip, and tie vertically. Repeat until the mixture is used up.

Add 1 bay leaf, the sprig of coriander and cumin to pan of water. Bring water to the boil, and dip tamales in water. Simmer for 1 hour, until contents are firm. When cooked, drain and serve hot.

Snacks

Plantain

Varieties of the banana include the Plantain, ('Musa paradisíaca'), or 'Plátano', a vegetable type of the common banana, many different types of which are cultivated in Cuba. 'Plátano Verde' is a green cooking banana, or plantain. It is less sweet, with a higher starch content, and larger than the familiar yellow banana. Plantain can be boiled, fried, or baked, and used as a vegetable, or dessert, depending how ripe they are. Bananas and plantain are high in energy and fibre, and contain potassium, folic acid, and minerals. They also contain vitamin B, some iron and calcium, and are said to prevent gastric ulcers. If you want potato chips with everything, whilst eating in a Cuban restaurant, ask for 'Papa Frita' or 'Saratoga'. 'Papa' is the local name for the potato. However, for an unusual snack with a drink, or side dish, ask for maraquita, or maduros, fried plantain crisps. Plantains contain even more calories than bananas, with 122 per 10 grams of fruit. The Cubans have a pet name for a foreigner who has fallen in love with Cuba, 'Aplantanado', 'gone native' or, literally - 'a plantain eater'!

Maraquita - Plantain Snack

4 ripe plantains, peeled, and sliced very thin
2 tsp salt
335ml (12 fl oz) salt water
deep fat fryer, one third filled with cooking oil

Soak plantain slices in salt water for 15 minutes. Remove slices and dry thoroughly. Heat the oil to 190ºC (375ºF). Place half plantain slices in frying basket. Lower gently into oil. Fry until crisp and golden, then fry remainder. Sprinkle crisps with salt and serve hot or cold.

Classic Cuban Cookery

Sunflower

Native to the Americas, the seeds of the sunflower ('Helianthus annus'), are a nutritious food in their own right, and are also the source of the highly useful oil. The Spanish name for this plant is 'girasol', or 'Girasol Silvestre', and the oil extracted from the 'pipas' (seeds) is called 'aceite de girasol'. The seeds have expectorant qualities, and can also be used as a diuretic, and a form of coffee is also made from the dried ground seeds. Sunflower buds can be boiled and eaten and the leaves used to be dried and smoked as a herbal tobacco. The plant can grow to twelve foot, and has a large head of seeds, surrounded by yellow petals. Their association with the sun led the Aztecs to revere the plant, to which they attributed special powers. Corn oil can be substituted for the sunflower oil in this typical Cuban side dish.

TOSTONES CON QUESO – CUBAN CHEESE TOASTIES

   4 green, vegetable plantains, peeled and thickly sliced
   5 tbs of sunflower oil
   3 tsp of garlic powder
   225g (8oz) cheese

Heat the oil in a frying pan to 180ºC (350ºF). Place plantain slices into the oil and cook for 2 minutes. Drain tostones on kitchen paper and then press each of the slices out flat using a cheese board. Bring oil up to 190ºC (375ºF). Sprinkle garlic powder onto the oil. Fry all the tostones once more, until golden brown. Drain again. Cut cheese into square slices, so they are the same size as tostones. Place cheese squares on each of the tostones. Place tostones on baking dish and melt cheese under hot grill.

Snacks

Relleno de Picadillo – Beef Burger Fillers

4 onions, peeled and finely chopped
3 garlic cloves, finely chopped
700g (1 1/2lbs) lean beef mince
75g (3oz) green olives, stoned and chopped
2 tbs olive oil
75g (3oz) raisins
110ml (4 fl oz) Gold rum
2 tbs capers
5 tbs tomato purée
1/2 tbs dried oregano
pinch of salt and ground black pepper
4 bun rolls, halved

Sauté onions in oil for 10 minutes. Add garlic and then the meat. Brown for around 5 minutes. Reduce heat and add rum. Add the rest of the ingredients and cook over a low heat for 10 minutes. Stir ingredients and season, mixing in the flavours. Spoon the cooked mixture into the bun rolls.

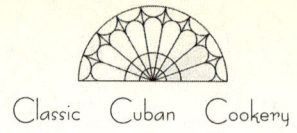

Classic Cuban Cookery

Empanadas – Cuban Meat and Vegetable Patties

Pastry:
450g (1lb) plain flour
2 tsp baking flour
1 tsp salt
75g (3oz) lard and butter mixed

Filling:
2 medium onions, chopped fine
2 raw potatoes, finely diced
450g (1lb) lean mince
3 tbs beef stock
1 egg, beaten with 1/2 tsp of milk
1 tomato, chopped
1 tbs raisins
1 tbs chopped green olives
1/2 tbs capers
1 hard boiled egg, chopped
1 tsp chilli powder and cumin seeds mixed.
150ml (1/4 pint) dry sherry
1 tsp soft brown sugar
25g (1oz) butter

Make a firm pastry with the first set of ingredients. Chill for 1 hour. Set aside tomatoes, onion, potatoes and meat. Mix rest of filling ingredients in large bowl. Melt cooking butter

Snacks

in pan. Add onion and tomato and cook for 5 minutes. Add mince and potatoes, and cook for a further 5 minutes. Add rest of ingredients, reduce heat, cook for 10 minutes then cool. Set mixture aside. Roll out the pastry to 4 mm thickness. Using a pastry cutter, cut out as many 15 cm rounds of pastry as possible. Place a small heap of filling in each of the rounds. Coat edges of pastry with water, and seal by pressing together. Place empanadas on baking dish and bake for 15 minutes in hot oven.

Turn heat down to 110°C (250°F) and bake for another 30-40 minutes. Serve when golden brown.

Enchilados

Depending on where you are in Latin America, 'enchilados' can mean different things. In Mexico, an 'enchilada' is a stuffed tortilla, and 'enchilada picante' means 'spicy hot'. It can mean 'seasoned with chilli' or 'bright red' or it can refer to a stew with a chilli sauce. In Cuba, 'enchilados' are stuffed tortilla snacks, or they can also refer to omelettes. 'Fajitas', another word for wraps, are a similar snack to the stuffed tortilla. 'Enchilado' fillings vary, but are usually fish, such as in the following recipe, made with shark steak or meat with a sauce.

ENCHILADOS TIBERON – SHARK MEAT SNACKS

450g (1lb) shark fillet
4 tortilla shells
1 tbs olive oil
1 medium onion, peeled and finely chopped
3 cloves garlic, finely chopped
2 Jalapeno chillies, seeded and finely chopped

Classic Cuban Cookery

1 sprig fresh coriander, chopped
175g (6oz) tomato purée
1 laurel leaf
1 1/2 tsp salt
1/4 tsp sugar
1/4 tsp pepper
1/4 tsp cumin seeds
1/4 tsp dried oregano
1 tsp vinegar
1 tsp dry white wine

Wash fish and cut into small pieces. Make a sauce in the pan with the oil, onion, garlic and chillies. Stir in the tomato purée and the coriander. Heat until bubbling and then turn the heat down and add the rest of the ingredients. Stir, and cook over a low heat for around 20 minutes. Spoon the cooked fish and sauce into the tortillas.

Classic Cuban Cookery

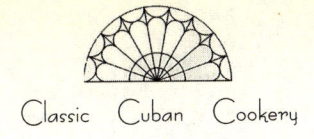

Salads

Classic Cuban Cookery

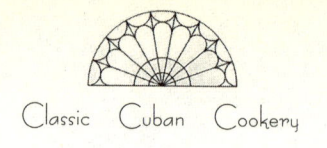

The Sevilla Hotel, Havana

The Sevilla Hotel originally opened its doors on 22 March 1908, and was refurbished and reopened in 1924 as the Sevilla Biltmore. This most elegant hotel, with its plush fittings and gracious decorations, complete with Spanish tiling and treasured statues was in fact the hotel featured in Graham Greene's novel, 'Our man in Havana'. Room 501 is made famous through Greene's work, as the venue for the meeting between spy-master Hawthorne and the carpet cleaner salesman.

The hotel boasts a panoply of famous real-life guests, including Caruso, Gloria Swanson, Lola Flores and Josephine Baker. Today, the hotel has several shops and two main restaurants, La Giralda and the Parrillada, as well as a roof-garden restaurant and four bars. One of these is the famous Bar Habana, which has wonderful views of the Morro Castle, and features a typically Cuban arcaded frontage. Behind the hotel, which is also renowned for its beautiful Sevillian Patio feature, is a large swimming pool.

'Our Man in Havana' was first published in 1958, after Greene had made several visits to Cuba. The clubs mentioned in his book, such as the Shanghai theatre are now long gone, but just behind the Sevilla Hotel is the legendary Sloppy Joe's. Abandoned since the 1950s, Havana's original 'Sloppy Joe's' bar dates from the mid-19th century and the building is in typically Havana Baroque, or neo-classical Colonial style. The bar itself was opened in around 1912, and Prohibition-buster, Joe Russell, opened a copycat Sloppy Joe's bar in Key West, Florida, in the late 1920s. From the 1920s to 50s, Havana Sloppy Joe's was a favourite meeting place for film stars like Errol Flynn, Gary Cooper, Spencer Tracy, Jimmy Durante, Lou Costello, Marlon Brando, Robert Taylor, Marlene Dietrich, Brigitte Bardot, Barbara Stanwyck and Ava Gardner. Jean Paul Sartre, Francoise Sagan and Ernest Hemingway were some of the writers that frequented the bar, along with musicians like Duke Ellington and Cab Calloway, and singers Frank Sinatra, Ginger Rogers, Eartha Kitt, Carmen Miranda and Nat King Cole. Heavyweight boxer Joe Louis drank in Sloppy Joe's, as did Meyer Lansky, Al Capone, 'Lucky' Luciano,

Frank Costello, Santos Trafficante and many more. Open 24 hours, never closing its doors, Sloppy Joe's was famous for its Planter's Punch, Daiquiris and inch-thick ham and cheese sandwiches made with rye bread.

Salads

Cuba grows a wide selection of standard salad ingredients, from tomatoes and spring onions, to letttuce and cucumber. However, Cuban salads, or 'ensaladas', can be presented somewhat differently to that which most visitors are used to. 'Ensalata mixta' can vary from diced vegetables, to a more conventional mixed salad. Tomato salads are often made with green tomatoes, served with an olive oil sauce. Cabbage and cucumber salad, Ensalada de pepinos y col, is chopped cabbage with very finely sliced cucumber, with olive oil, and other unusual salads are made with the curiously shaped chayote, or chunks of the avocado pear.

Somewhat unusually, Cuban salads are sometimes made with vegetables, such cold, diced potatoes, turnips, beetroot, carrots and french beans, or peas. Side salads are commonly served with a main dish and may consist of just sliced tomatoes, or a few lettuce leaves and radishes. Onions are sometimes served on their own as a side salad with olive oil dressing. One typical, delicious salad dish is cold Moros y Cristiones, translated as 'Moors and Christians', a traditional side dish to rice and black beans. This is a salad of chopped, fresh coriander, onions, garlic and olive oil, drizzled with lime juice.

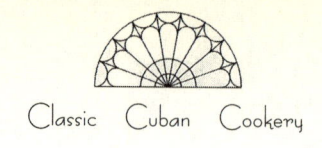

Chayote

The native Chayote ('*Sechium edule*') is also known as 'Caimato', 'Choko' or 'Christophene', is named from the Arawak chayote, which is in turn derived from the Aztec word, 'chayotl'. Chayote was widely cultivated in Aztec Mexico, from whence it arrived in Cuba. It is a member of the same family as squash, marrow and pumpkin family (Cucurbitaceae). The fruit is light green and pear-shaped with deeply-ridged skin, and it has a single, round flat seed. The fruit should be boiled before eating, and peeled only after cooking. It tastes rather like marrow, and can be served in a number of ways, either hot, cold, as a vegetable or in salads. The chayote contains some vitamin C, its tuberous roots are an excellent source of starch, and the fruits have just 31 calories per 100 grams. Chayote is available in most supermarkets in the exotic fruit and vegetable section.

ENSALATA MIXTA A LA CUBANA – CUBAN MIXED SALAD

1 chayote, coarsely chopped
1 avocado, peeled, stoned, and sliced lengthways
1/2 cucumber, peeled and finely sliced
1/2 small honeydew melon, peeled and cubed
2 courgettes, sliced and cooked for 5 minutes, then cooled
1 tomato, chopped
1 sweet green bell pepper, seeded and chopped

Dressing:
juice of 2 limes
3 tbs olive oil

Salads

2 tbs vinegar from pickled chillies
1/4 tsp cumin powder
1/4 tsp paprika
pinch of salt and pepper

Mix all ingredients for the dressing together except paprika. Combine all salad ingredients in a bowl. Cover with dressing and toss well. Leave to stand in cool place. Before serving, sprinkle salad with paprika.

Tuna Pear (Prickly pear)

The Prickly Pear ('Optunia ficus-indica'), also known as tuna, Indian fig, or 'higo chumbo', derives from the Americas and grows on the opuntia cactus, commonly known as 'nopal'. English speakers might well translate this as 'No Pal', for the hairy spines which can be very painful! The oval, red-green fruit has a delicious red flesh, which can be eaten raw, or made into a fine jam. Lime juice brings out its delicate flavour. To gather tuna in the wild, knock the ripe fruit (which should have turned from green to yellowish-pink) from the cactus with a stick. To remove the spines, roll the fruit on the ground with a foot or a stick. The fruit can be prepared by holding it down with a fork, and cutting off both ends. Next, skin the fruit by cutting it lengthways and peeling the skin off to reveal the flesh. An excellent jelly can be made with 8 prickly pears, sliced and cooked along with the pulp of 6 passion fruit, the juice of 2 oranges and a little water. Add 10g dissolved gelatine, and cook until stiff. Strain the jelly and cool. Serve in glasses, topped with whipped cream. The young leaves of the prickly pear, known as 'nopalitos', can be used in stews and in salads.

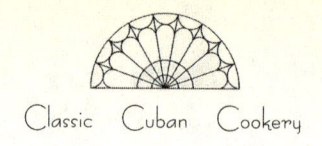

Ensalada Aguacate y Tomate – Avocado and Tomato Salad

    1 avocado, peeled, stoned and diced
    6 medium sized ripe tomatoes, sliced
    1 sweet green bell pepper, blanched and diced
    1 large spanish onion
    2 spring onions, chopped finely
    1 tbs chopped fresh coriander
    1 tsp seeded red chilli, finely chopped,
    1 tsp coriander seeds
    6 tbs white wine
    3 tbs olive oil
    pinch of salt
    pinch of fresh ground black pepper

Slice onion into rings, and blanch in a little water. Strain onions and add sliced tomatoes and diced pepper to pan. Add wine, oil and coriander seeds to pan. Simmer for 30 minutes, or until liquid is reduced by half. Turn out mixture, strain off liquid into cup, and let cool. In a bowl, combine avocado, chilli, and spring onions. Mix in the tomatoes and onion. Season with salt and pepper. Pour liquid from tomatoes and onions over salad. Sprinkle with chopped coriander. Serve very cold.

Ensalada Espanola – Spanish Salad

    450g (1lb) large, red-green tomatoes
    1 large spanish onion

Salads

    1 sweet green bell pepper
    1 tbs mixed herbs
    2 tbs white wine
    6 tsp olive oil
    pinch of salt
    pinch of fresh ground black pepper
    1/4 tsp pimenton (Spanish paprika)

Combine wine and oil to make French dressing. Scald tomatoes, skin, and slice vertically. Cut the onion in thin rings. Slice the pepper in rings and cut out pith and seeds. Boil both the onions and pepper in water for 1 minute. Remove from heat and drain. Mix onions and pepper together in a bowl. Season with salt and pepper. Pour french dressing over salad. Sprinkle with herbs and pimenton, or cayenne pepper.

Ensalada Elote y Pimiento – Maize and Pepper Salad

    225g (8oz) fresh maize kernels
    1 large sweet red bell pepper, seeded and sliced
    10 small pickled onions, halved
    3 tbs white wine
    4 tbs olive oil
    4 black olives, stoned and quartered
    juice of one lime
    1/4 tsp salt
    1/2 tsp pimenton

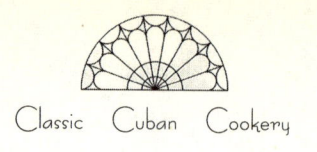

Cut each pepper slice into half. Boil the maize and peppers with salt until kernels are soft. Drain and place maize and peppers in a bowl. Mix in the olives and pickled onions. Pour over the lime juice and let cool. Mix wine and olive oil together for dressing. Spoon dressing over salad. Dust lightly with pimenton, or cayenne pepper.

The Royal Palm

More than 90 varieties of palm can be found in Cuba. Some of these were introduced, but the indigenous and stately Royal Palm, or 'Palma Real' ('Roystonea Regia') is the Cuban national tree, and is featured on the Cuban coat of arms. The tall, silvery-grey trunk supports a profusion of leaves that burst from the very top of the tree. New leaves sprout every new moon from the top of the trunk, which can grow up to 30 metres in height. Every year, clusters of creamy white flowers give way to fruit, which hang in great bunches from the palm fronds, exuding their heavy, sugary scent. Bees, bats and hummingbirds are attracted to the nectar, and the Cubans harvest palm honey from the bees feeding off Royal Palm nectar. Cuba is a major exporter of honey ('meile'). The fruit, which grow in clusters from the crown of the tree, are small and purple and rich in oils and carbohydrates, and the seeds, known as 'paplmiche' are used as animal feed. The jelly-like pulp surrounding the seed of the Royal Palm can be used in fruit salads.

Prior to the Cuban revolution, the heart of the Royal palm tree was used in cold dishes, such as 'millionaire's salad', or 'palmito'. This practice was forbidden, as cutting the heart out of the palm can kill the majestic tree. Now, palm heart comes from other varieties of palm, such as the Cabbage Palm, which can grow to a height of 100 foot. This palm has a straight trunk, crowned by a topknot of fronds. Palm hearts have a taste similar to a mixture of artichoke, asparagus and avocado, and if cut when the shoots are very young, can be eaten raw, but palm hearts are normally cooked in salted water.

Salads

ENSALATA MILLIONARIO – MILLIONAIRE'S PALM HEART SALAD

450g (1lb) prepared palm hearts, coarsely chopped
110g (4oz) small mushrooms, cleaned and sliced
4 black olives, stoned and halved
4 green olives, stoned and halved
1 sweet green bell pepper, seeded and cut into thin strips
1 tbs chopped chives
1 tsp fresh chopped parsley
2 medium potatoes, cooked, cooled and diced
225g (8oz) shelled prawns
110g (4oz) canned tuna meat, broken small

Dressing:
175ml (6 fl oz) mayonnaise
2 tbs lime juice
2 tbs pickled chilli vinegar
1 tbs olive oil
1/4 tsp salt
1/2 tsp ground black pepper
1 tsp paprika
1/2 tsp prepared mustard

Prepare dressing by beating mayonnaise, mustard, and paprika. Beat in salt and pepper, lime juice, oil and vinegar. Pour dressing over salad ingredients in a large bowl and toss well.

Classic Cuban Cookery

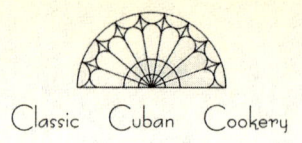

Classic Cuban Cookery

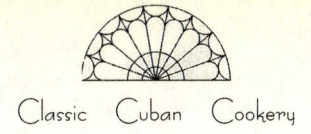

Soups

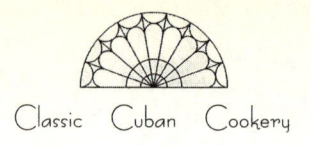

The Inglaterra Hotel, Havana

The neo-baroque Inglaterra Hotel was built in the 1870s by Fransisco Fernandez, an engineer in the Spanish Colonial Army, and is one of Cuba's oldest and most prestigious hotels. Completed in 1875, it was opened later that year on 23rd December. At one stage it was known as the Café Louvre and was one of the most popular meeting places of mid 19th century Havana. Architecturally, the Inglaterra is a typically Colonial edifice, with columned portals and repousse iron balconies, which include the famous 'Louvre steps'. Colonial soldiers fired on Cuban conspirators on this sidewalk in 1869 and the Spaniard, Nicolas Estevanez broke his sword on the hotel steps protesting against the execution of eight Cuban students in 1871. A plaque on the hotel wall commemorates this event. In 1879 Jose Marti gave a speech from the hotel's doorway and, in 1889 General Antonio Maceo stayed at the hotel for five months, using it as his headquarters.

The Inglaterra, with its neo-classical facade and mudejar Spanish-Arab interior, has 84 rooms and has been favoured by many visiting celebrities such as Enrico Caruso, Sarah Bernardt, the Cuban chess-player Jose Raul Capablanca, Spanish playwright Jacinto Benavente, and many politicians. The lobby features early Spanish ceramics, Alicante mosaics, ornamental ironwork, Spanish-style window grills, stained glass windows, heraldic symbols, and carved wooden doors. The highlight in the foyer is a golden statue, which was inspired by Bizet's Carmen. The hotel is the home to the Colonial Restaurant, Sevillana bar, Terraza grill-bar, two shops and a central patio, and is now a national monument.

Soups

Soups

In the early days of the New World, Spanish colonists were forbidden to cultivate grapes and olives, in case it deprived Spanish merchants of an income. Thus, both olive oil and wine were shipped to Cuba on a regular basis in return for hides, tallow, timber and other agricultural produce. The Spanish brought a number of European recipes with them to Cuba, one of which was sofrito, a word meaning lightly fried, or sauteed. This refers to a basic cooking sauce. The Spanish version is made by frying sausage, ham, herbs, onions, garlic, and salt and pepper, in olive oil. The Cuban sofrito is a paste of finely chopped garlic, onions and peppers fried in oil, and most Cuban cooks begin preparing savoury dishes by first making a sofrito. The Cuban version of the dish usually has the addition of an aromatic oil, such as peanut, maize or olive oil, and is coloured and flavoured with annatto seeds. Tomatoes, sweet peppers and fresh coriander are also usually added. The sauce is often thickened with the addition of finely ground peanuts, or grated, hard-boiled, egg yolk. This forms the basis of many Cuban main meals, soups, and stews. Sofritos can also be used as a complement to main dishes, or is even eaten as a savoury spread.

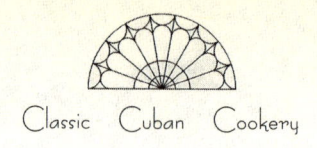

Sofrito

2 spanish onions, finely chopped
1 large green bell pepper, seeded and finely chopped
1 medium red bell pepper, seeded and finely chopped
6 cloves garlic, pressed
2 tsp pimenton or paprika
275g (10oz) tomato purée
1 tbs fresh chopped coriander
1 tsp dried oregano
1 tsp red wine vinegar
1 tsp annatto seeds
110ml (4 fl oz) olive oil

Cook annatto seeds in oil until the oil is coloured. Discard the annatto seeds. Sautee onions, garlic, and peppers in oil until onions are gold. Add pimenton and cook for 5 minutes. Add tomatoes, coriander, oregano and vinegar. Cook for ten minutes, stirring regularly. Hot stock and soup or stew ingredients can now be added if desired.

Arrowroot

Used as a thickening agent in confectionery, arrowroot is obtained from the native plant known by the Arawaks as 'aranuta' or 'flour root'. Its name in Spanish is arrurruz (Maranta arundinacea). Arrowroot powder is made from the long, white spiky root, or rhizome, which is grated, sifted, washed and dried. It is used as a thickener for sauces, soups and puddings and is easily digested and very nutritious. Just a teaspoon of arrowroot, added to this delicious soup, gives it pastel colouring, and slight thickening.

Soups

Sopa de Jengibre y Aguacate – Ginger and Avocado Soup

    35g (1 1/2 oz) fresh grated ginger
    110g (4oz) butter
    1 medium onion, finely chopped
    1 large avocado, peeled, stoned and mashed
    450ml (16 fl oz) chicken stock
    1 shallot, finely chopped
    1 celery stalk, finely chopped
    50ml single cream
    1 tsp arrowroot, dissolved in an eggcup of water
    1 tsp salt
    1 tsp black pepper
    1 spring onion, finely chopped

Saute onion, shallot, celery and ginger in butter for 2 minutes. Add avocado flesh and chicken stock, whisking to mix ingredients. Simmer slowly, stirring, for around 15 minutes. Stir in the arrowroot mixture. Add salt, pepper and cream, stirring the mixture for 2 minutes. Chill soup and garnish with chopped spring onion.

Okra

The Okra plant was brought over from West Africa (where it is known as Gumbo) in the 17th century, to supplement the slaves' diet. Okra (Hibiscus esculentus) is known locally as quimbombo, or kimbombo, and the plant grows to around 4 to 6 feet in height. The soft, tapering, green pod is edible, and can grow to 5 inches (13 centimetres) in length, although there is a shorter variety. The pods are actually the aromatic beans of a plant in the mallow family. Because the pods are mucilaginous, they are used whole, as a thickener in soups and stews. The pods have many edible seeds within, and they are rich in vitamins B and C as well as various minerals. Okra is also low in calories, with just 42 calories per 100 grams. Okra, also known as 'bhindi' and 'ladies fingers' should be smooth and green when picked or bought and should be used quickly, as they brown within a few days of picking. A delicious soup can be made from eddoes, thickened by the addition of okra.

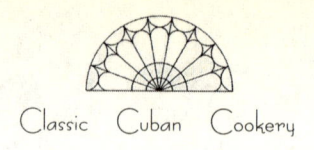

SOPA KIMBOMBO – OKRA AND EDDOE SOUP

450g (1lb) peeled eddoes
6 okra pods
225g (8oz) of salt pork
1 medium onion, sliced
1 tbs butter
1 large tomato, blanched, skinned, and chopped
1/2 tsp dried thyme
1/2 tsp dried marjoram
dash of Worcestershire sauce
2.25 l (4 pints) water
pinch of salt and pepper
150ml (1/4 pint) single cream

Soak salt meat overnight. Remove and cut into cubes. Cook eddoes, okra, and salt meat until meat is tender. Remove meat and set aside, keeping hot. Add all other ingredients and simmer until mixture is smooth. Remove from heat and purée soup mixture. Add meat to soup and heat in pan until bubbling. Remove from heat. Serve with a tablespoon of cream poured onto each helping.

Soups

Peanuts

The peanut has been a major food source in the South America and the Caribbean for at least 3,500 years. Pottery jars made in the shape of peanuts, and decorated with pictures of the nuts have been found in South America, dating back to 1500BC, and the Incas were often buried with jars full of groundnuts. The Portuguese introduced the peanut (also known as the groundnut, ground pea or monkey nut) to West Africa from South America in the 16th century. This edible tuber spread back to the Caribbean, reintroduced by the West African slaves. Part of the legume family of vegetables, Arachis hypoganea thrives in quite arid conditions and is an ideal cash crop for this part of the world. The kernels are planted between April and May each year, and the flowers of the young plant send down white shoots, known as pegs back down into the soil. The pegs develop the familiar peanuts in their hard shells after about 2 months. The peanut is an annual plant with a yearly crop. Once pulled from the ground, peanuts are left out in the sun to dry. Between 25-50% moisture is contained in the fresh nut, which must be reduced by sun-drying to 10% or less in order for them to be preserved. The nuts are dried in two to four days, and then they are ready for storing.

Peanuts are a very high source of protein and are an integral part of western vegetarian diets and mny Afro-Cuban dishes. Once ounce of peanuts contains as much protein as an egg, and they are high in healthy mono- and polyunsaturated fats. Groundnut oil is also widely used in cooking, although most Cubans prefer the slightly rancid taste of palm oil. Products made from the nut include refined oil, margarine, and soap, which is made from lower grade oil. Care should be taken when cooking dishes containing peanuts as there are some people that have violent and dangerous allergic reactions to peanuts.

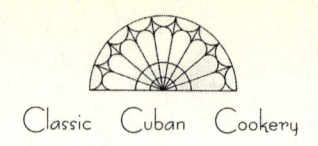

Sopa de Mani Arco – Rainbow Peanut Soup

150g (5oz) finely ground roasted peanuts or peanut butter
2 tomatoes, chopped
1 sweet red bell pepper, seeded and chopped
1 onion, finely chopped
2 cloves garlic, finely chopped
1.2 l (2 pints) stock or water
2 tbs freshly chopped coriander
2 tbs groundnut oil
1 tsp annatto seeds
1 Habanero chilli, seeded and finely chopped

Heat annatto seeds in oil to flavour and colour. Discard seeds. Fry onion, pepper and garlic in oil until soft. Purée all ingredients, except the peanuts and coriander. Fry the mixture, together with the peanuts, stirring for 3 minutes. Add all ingredients, except coriander, to stock or water in pan. Cover, and cook over a low heat for 15 minutes. Serve, garnished with coriander.

Corn

Corn, also known as Indian corn or maize, is a native to the New World and has been cultivated in the Americas since 2000BC. Maize probably spread to Cuba through the trading Mayas from nearby Yucatan in Mexico. In Amerindian times, it was known as mais *and is now called* maíz, *or sometimes* elote *in Cuba. Maize is now widely grown in Cuba and forms the basis for many dishes. There are three main varieties; sweet corn is the most widely used, and is often known as green corn, because the cob is picked before* it ripens. Sweet corn is eaten raw, boiled or roasted. Dent corn is the source of cornflour and popcorn earns its name from the sound made by the corn kernels when they are heated. Sweetcorn makes a nourishing and aromatic soup, to which chorizo sausage is sometimes added.

Sopa de Elote – Maize Soup

Corn kernels from 8 maize ears
570ml (1 pint) chicken stock
2 lightly beaten eggs
2 tbs fine chopped fresh coriander
150ml (1/4 pint) single cream
1 sweet green bell pepper, chopped
4 garlic cloves, finely chopped
110ml (4 fl oz) peanut oil
225ml (8 oz) tomato purée
1 butternut squash, diced fine
1 pinch of both salt and black pepper

Blend corn with stock in processor. Blend rest of ingredients, except eggs, cream and coriander.
Mix the two together in cooking pan. Simmer mix over low heat for 5 minutes, stirring in cream. Work mixture through sieve, return to pan and add salt and pepper. Simmer, and stir quarter of mixture into beaten eggs. Stir mixture back into the pan and cook for 2 minutes. Serve garnished with coriander.

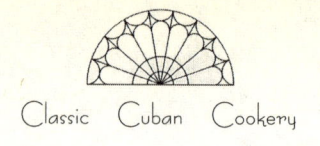

Breadnut

The native New World Breadnut should not to be confused with the imported breadfruit. This is the yellow fruit of a tall straight tree, common in the Caribbean. Breadnuts are either boiled or roasted and flour can also be made from the fruit. Bread can be baked from this flour, and it can be used to thicken soups and stews. The edible part of the nut is the kernal, and this has a taste similar to hazelnuts.

Guarana

The guarana nut, which grows on a form of liana vine has the highest caffeine content of any nut. The tri-celled fruit contains a seed similar to a horse chestnut and before it can be used, it must be roasted for about six hours. The Amerindians first used it as a medicine in the form of a tonic to cure headaches, neuralgia and nowadays it is used in many energy and tonic drinks. Guarana is an appetite suppressant and the oil, guaranine is thought to be an aphrodisiac. A recipe, dating back to Arawak times, describes a 'pasta guarana', which is a paste of ground guarana nut mixed with cassava flour. This paste is used to thicken soups and stews.

Palm Chestnut

The palm chestnut, a native of the New World was once one of the staples in the diet of the Amerindians. The nut is a single seed, surrounded by an edible pulp, which tastes like coconut, and the oil-rich nuts can also be eaten once they have been boiled in salted water for about three hours. Once ground, the nuts can be used to add flavour and body to soups and stews.

Soups

Out on the cattle ranches of the Camaguey region of Cuba, where great plains roll out to the horizon, rodeos are sometimes held on the local Saint's Day. The climax of the celebrations may include a barbecue with a difference. Roast suckling pig is the favourite victim for this ancient method of preparation, which dates back to the times of the Tiano Amerindians, who named it after their raised resting platforms, known as barbacoas. First, a large pit is dug in the ground and lined with either banana leaves, or long spiky agave leaves. The pit is half-filled with stones and a fire is built over the top, which heats the stones. The slaughtered pig is put in a dish and flavoured with annato seeds, ginger, onions, peppercorns, garlic and oregano, then wrapped in pimento and banana leaves. Root vegetables, such as jucca and sweet potatoes are placed around the pig, and the dish is lowered onto the stones, after the fire has died down. The pit is then filled with more banana leaves and soil and sealed. In 3-4 hours, the feast is ready, and the pork is often served with a green bean soup, such as the one in the following recipe.

SOPA DE FRIJOLES TIERNOS − FRESH GREEN BEAN SOUP

450g (1lb) fresh green French beans
2 medium onions, finely chopped
1.5 litres (2 1/2 pints) stock
55ml (2 fl oz) olive oil
1/2 tsp dried oregano
Pinch of salt and pepper

Fry onions in the oil until soft. Set aside. Simmer the beans in the stock for 10 minutes. Remove beans from the stock and purée them. Mix the bean purée and onions into the stock. Add salt, pepper and oregano to taste. Serve hot.

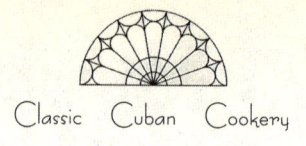

Beans

The most popular of the many beans used in Cuban cookery are the red and black varieties of kidney bean. The red kidney bean, or colorado bean has a buttery flavour and is commonly used in refried beans, and the black variety, or bayos, is more commonly cooked with rice. Haricot beans, also known as the common white bean or blanco are used in baked beans and stews. Pinto beans and the green haricot or flageolet are not widely used in Cuban cookery, but the American and Creole favourite, black-eyed beans are often used in pork stews.

Sopa Frijoles Bayos mi Casita - Black Bean Soup

　　450g (1lb) dried black beans, soaked overnight
　　2 bay leaves
　　175ml (6 fl oz) olive oil
　　1 sweet red bell pepper, seeded and chopped coarsely
　　1 sweet green bell pepper, seeded and chopped coarsely
　　4 shallots, sliced finely
　　1 1/2 tbs soft brown sugar
　　2 tbs fresh, finely chopped coriander
　　5 pints water
　　juice of 3 oranges
　　juice of 1 lime
　　2 cloves garlic, crushed
　　1 small onion, sliced fine
　　1 tbs white rum
　　1 tbs sherry

Soups

pinch salt
1 tsp dried oregano
1/4 tsp ground cumin
1/2 tbs fresh root ginger, finely chopped

Boil the beans in the water with bay leaves. Reduce to simmer, and cook for 3 1/2 hours until tender. Saute the shallots, peppers, ginger and garlic in the oil. When tender, add the coriander and sugar. Fry for 30 seconds. Add lime and orange juice, rum, sherry, oregano and cumin. Cook for 2 minutes and add salt. Remove bay leaves from beans and add sauteed mixture to beans. Stir and serve hot.

Sopa Frijoles Francisco – Franciscan Red Bean Soup

350g (12 oz) dried red beans, boiled for 10 minutes
1 medium onion, chopped
2 celery stalks, chopped
175g (6 oz) salt pork, cubed
6 serrano peppers, chopped
1/2 tsp Tabasco sauce
2 cloves garlic, crushed
125 ml Anejo rum
125 ml sour cream
1 bay leaf
25g (1 oz) butter
1.75 litres (3 pints) water

Classic Cuban Cookery

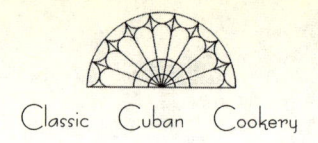

Boil beans, onion, celery, pork, bay, peppers, sauce and garlic. Reduce heat and simmer for 2 hours. Discard bay leaf. Put soup in casserole dish, and blend in butter and half the rum. Cover and bake in oven for 1 hour. Stir in rest of rum, and top with cream before serving.

Classic Cuban Cookery

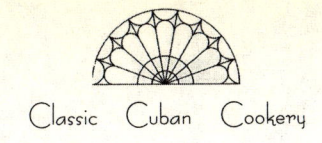

Meat Dishes

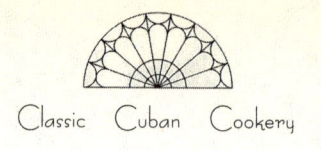

The Morro Castle, Havana

El Forteleza de los Tres Santos Reyes Magos de Morro was originally a small white lookout tower, built on the instructions of Governor Diego de Mazariegos in 1563. The Morro is a familiar symbol of Havana City and is made from great blocks of coral rock. It is built on an elevated headland - which is what 'morro' means - at the mouth of Havana Harbour. The fort is dominated by the 1844 lighthouse which is 24m (76ft) high and the light can be seen 80km (50 miles) away - almost to Key West!
Extensively damaged by a mine during the English onslaught in 1762, when Havana was taken and occupied by the Earl of Albemarle's forces, the castle was rebuilt in 1763. At its highest point the walls are 60 metres above sea level, thirty metres high and five metres wide. Across the drawbridge, which spans the deep moat, are the great wooden doors and a narrow, arched passage which leads out into the castle's interior. Inside its thick walls, the Morro is a maze of cobbled passageways, embrasures with slits for guns, sentry boxes, stairways and ramps which lead to patios, powder magazines and battlements. The main fort is built on stepped ramparts containing chambers, galleries, gun emplacements and dungeons, some of which have been converted to house a restaurant. Sixty cannons still point out to sea, including the huge 'Twelve Apostle' guns which were often employed against pirate ships and those of the English Naval forces who captured the castle in 1762. Los Doce Apostoles restaurant in the castle is named after the guns, and is located in the Bateria del Sol. It serves Cuban criolla food. Open from midday until midnight. The Taberna Castillo de los Tres Reyes del Morro Inn offers a selection of drinks. There is also a juice bar, nightclub, museum and souvenir shop.

Meat Dishes

Meat in Cuba

Cuba's farm animals are raised on entirely natural produce, as artificial feeds are too expensive to import, so all meat in Cuba is organic. The favourite meat on the Cuban table is undoubtedly pork, although chicken is also popular. Cattle are also farmed in Havana and Gamaguey provinces - in the 1980s, Fidel Castro's elder brother, Ramon, developed the famous F-1 strain of cattle in conjunction with Oxford University's agricultural department in England. It was Ramon, in the early 1980s, who introduced the author to the traditionally Cuban style of barbecuing meat, on his ranch in Picadura. This breed was developed especially for the Cuban climate, as few strains of cattle thrive in the Caribbean weather. The breed is noted for being a good milk producer, and an excellent beef cow.

There is a reason for the Cuban's preference for meat, rather than fish. During the grim days of the Batista dictatorship, the Cuban population was brought almost to starvation point by the excesses of the few, very rich sugar barons, ranchers and officials. Food distribution was tightly controlled, and the majority of the population was forced to the sea to supplement their meagre allocations. Luckily, the Caribbean and Atlantic waters around Cuba's 6,000 kilometre coastline team with fish of more than 900 varieties, as well as crustaceans. Forced for decades to resort to a diet of fish, fish acquired the stigma of being a 'poor man's dish'. Ever since the 1959 revolution, the people of Cuba have had more access to meat and will invariably choose meat in preference to fish, given the choice.

However, in the resort areas of Cuba, there is a wide range of international foods. Cuban dishes can be modified on tourist hotel menus, as there is the perception that visitors favour bland food. In Cuba there is the opportunity to try a variety of exotic meats, including crocodile tail, which comes form a large crocodile farm near the Zapata swamp peninsular, in Matazas province. Turtle meat is also generally on offer in tourist outlets, although the Cuban kitchen draws the line at the rare manatee or sea-cow. There are a *number of unusual game birds, which also find their way into the Cuban pot, like Yaguasa, pigeon, guinea fowl, quail, a number of migratory ducks and the local partridge. Both chicken and duck are bred in large numbers on co-operative farms throughout the country, and rabbit might sometimes appear on the menu. Lamb is not generally used in Cuban cooking, but is available in tourist resorts and in the cities. Goats are raised in Cuba, and wild boar is a particular favourite for barbecues. There are several herds of deer on the island, which regularly fall prey to the hunter's rifle, when in season.*

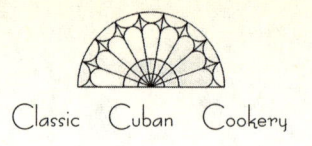

Milk products include locally made butter, which is generally unsalted, and cheese. Unfortunately collective farming and co-operatives under a socialist system did nothing for the entrepreneurial spirit when it comes to cheese production. Cuba's dairies churn out a passable variety of hard cheddar like cheese, but most cheese production is of the processed variety.

Meat Dishes

In the early days of the Spanish Main, Cuba's coasts were the haunt of numerous pirates, who would prey on treasure galleons heading for Europe. Pirates would also raid settlements, rustling the livestock. Cattle and hogs would run loose on offshore islands, and the outlaws would preserve this meat in salt, pack it in barrels and sell it to passing ships for the journey home. This meat was unpalatable, and needed to be washed in the precious fresh water supply before it could be eaten. The buccaneers soon found a better way of preserving the meat by smoking it over fires. This process was known as 'boucaning', which is where the name buccaneers comes from.

They also learnt how to cure meat using spices and chillies, which the Amerindians had been doing for centuries. Chilli peppers contain an antibacterial agent and are rich in vitamin C. This process is used today in Cuba and Jamaica, where the meat is known as jerky.

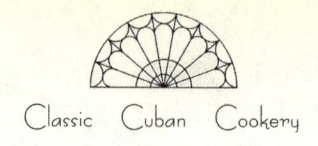

Allspice

Allspice is an indigenous Cuban spice, which has been used since before Columbus' time. The Spanish named it 'pimentia' as it resembled the pepper plant of Asia. The allspice bush bears a tiny berry which is sundried and ground. It is commonly used in pickling, along with dried chillies, mustard seeds, cloves, coriander, and ginger. It is also used as a flavouring for both sweet and savoury foods, such soups, meat dishes and cakes. The aromatic oil of allspice, is used in Bay Rum, perfumes, and soap-making. Medicinally, allspice is used in the treatment of chills and colds.

'Ropa Vieja', literally translated as 'old woman's clothes' is so-called because of the shredded beef used in this local recipe. It is the richness of this flavoursome concoction that imparts an almost South American flavour to this traditional Cuban dish.

Ropa Vieja – 'Old Woman's Clothes' (Cuban Stew)

900g (2lb) steak, minced or ground
1 large onion, chopped
2 carrots, peeled and sliced
2 cloves garlic, finely chopped
4 tomatoes, blanched, peeled and chopped
3 sweet red bell peppers chopped
50g (2oz) stem ginger, peeled and finely chopped
2 Jalapeno chillies, finely chopped
1 bay leaf
1 tbs capers
1/4 tsp cinnamon
1/4 tbs allspice

Meat Dishes

1 tsp fresh chopped oregano
1 tsp soft brown sugar
1 tsp salt and pinch of pepper
2 tbs olive oil
570ml (1 pint) water
225g (8oz) rice

Put steak, half the onions, bay leaf, sugar and salt in water. Simmer in pan for 1 1/2 hours, until meat is tender. Reserve the stock. Remove meat and cool. Cut, or shred into very thin strips. Sauté remaining onions, garlic, chillies, ginger, in oil. Add pepper and peppercorns. Stir in tomatoes, carrots, allspice, and cinnamon. Cook until the mixture becomes thick. Add meat and the stock, and cook until well heated. Serve on bed of rice.

Bay

Bay, or Bay Laurel ('Laurus nobilis'), was also one of the first herbs to be brought from Europe. The Spanish name for bay, is laurel. Bay leaves are a narcotic, an excitant, and are used in cures for colic and hysteria. The oil in its leaves and berries, has a warm, penetrating aroma, and is used in perfumes.

In 1791, around 27,000 sugar planters and their families escaped from a revolution in neighbouring Haiti to settle in Cuba. Most remained in the region around Santiago de Cuba, where the climate is hotter. The French had ruled Haiti until the revolution, when the plantation slaves went on the rampage. The main diet of these slaves, who originated mostly from the Congo in Africa, was 'Congri'. This is a thick creole casserole which was adapted by the Cubans, who added their favourite hot chilli seasoning and served it on a bed of rice. Congri is a favourite of the Santiagueros, or the people of Santiago de Cuba Province. Red beans are known as 'Frijoles Colorados' in Cuba.

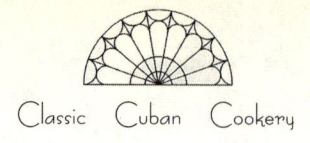

Congri Santiago – Creole Stew

The beans have to be soaked in water for at least ten hours. Wash hands carefully after slicing the chillies.
Serves 6.

450g (1lb) dried red beans, covered in water and soaked overnight
450g (1lb) offcuts of pork, or salt belly of pork, roughly diced
225g (8oz) bacon rashers, roughly chopped
225g (8oz) pork sausages, roughly diced
1 large onion, sliced
6 shallots, cut in quarters
2 carrots, sliced
2 garlic cloves, crushed
225g (8oz) red tomatoes, blanched, peeled and quartered
2 celery stalks, chopped
2 Habanero chillies, sliced small
2 Pimiento caps, sliced small
1.75l (3 pints) stock, or water
1 tbs tomato purée
3 tbs virgin olive oil
150ml (1/4 pint) dark rum (anejo)
1 bouquet garni
1 bay leaf
1/4 tsp black pepper
900g (2lb) plain white medium grained rice

Meat Dishes

2 tbs chopped parsley
12 wedges of lime, or lemon

Wash the soaked beans in a colander under the tap. Put them in a large pan or casserole. Add 1.2 l (2 1/2 pints) of water, and bring slowly to the boil. Simmer for 1 1/2 hours. Put the pork, bacon, sausage in a separate pan and cook them in the stock, or water, for around an hour. Drain the beans and discard water. Drain and save the water from the meat. Heat oil in the pan in which the meat was cooked in. Cook onion, shallots, carrots, tomatoes and celery for 5 minutes. Add tomato purée, beans, bouquet garni, bay leaf, rum, pepper. Add chillies, pimiento, garlic, rum and water which meat cooked in. Cover ingredients with cold water. Bring to the boil, then add the pork, bacon, and sausage pieces. Add pimiento, simmer for 1 hour, or until meat is tender. Prepare the rice, by boiling. Heat plates carefully. Add the chillies, garlic and tomatoes, to the stew mixture. Simmer for 1/2 hour. The stew should now be a rich, thick mixture - if it is too thick, add a little extra water. Remove bouquet garni and bay leaf, and season congri to taste. Serve in a deep casserole, and ladle out onto a bed of rice. Garnish with a sprinkling of parsley and two lemon wedges.

Breadfruit

The breadfruit, ('Artocarpus altilis'), or 'Fruto del Pan', was initially suggested as a supplement to the Caribbean diet by Captain Cook. Breadfruit was brought to the Caribbean from Polynesia by Captain William Bligh in 1793. Although rich in starch, this diet lacked vitamins, but the breadfruit contains 81 calories per 100 grams.
The breadfruit tree grows to around 60 feet (18 metres) in height and is part of the mulberry family. The fibrous bark has many uses, and breadfruit trees generally produce around 50 fruit, about 8 inches across, and weighing about 4lbs, although some fruit has

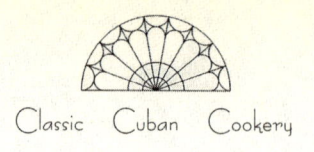

been recorded at 10lbs. The breadfruit seeds taste like chestnuts, but the seedless variety of the fruit, known as the yellow heart is considered best for cooking. The fruit is usually picked before it fully ripens, when it is yellow-green in colour. The flesh looks a little like fresh bread, hence its name, and it is very starchy, and although it is low in vitamin A, it is a good source of other vitamins. It is very versatile, and can be baked, roasted or boiled. The flesh has a faint taste of banana, and when sliced thinly and baked, breadfruit makes excellent vegetable chips. Breadfruit is often stuffed with a meat filling and when cooked whole makes a nourishing meal in itself.

Fruto Del Pan Disecado – Stuffed Breadfruit

1 large breadfruit
350g (12oz) minced beef
110g (4oz) minced pork
1 medium onion
2 shallots, finely chopped
1 medium tomato, chopped
1 tbs tomato purée
1 clove garlic, finely chopped
2 tbs maize oil
dash Worcestershire sauce
pinch of salt and pepper

Peel breadfruit and parboil in salted water. Allow to cool. Fry onions, shallots, garlic and tomato in oil until soft. Add purée, sauce, meat, salt and pepper to the mixture. Cook meat mixture until almost brown. From the stalk end of the breadfruit, cut out the core. Scoop out a little of the pulp, and fill cavity with mixture.

Bake for 50 minutes in a moderate oven until golden brown.

Carnicero – Cuban Meat Loaf

    900g (2lb) minced pork
    1 large onion, chopped
    4tbs salsa habanero or tabasco sauce
    75g (3oz) breadcrumbs
    1 egg, beaten
    2 tbs mustard powder
    110ml (4 fl oz) tomato purée
    2 tbs malt vinegar
    2 tbs brown sugar
    125ml pineapple juice
    1/2 tsp dried rosemary
    2 tbs Anejo rum
    275ml (1/2 pint) water
    pinch salt and pepper

Mix pork, onion, chilli sauce, egg, breadcrumbs, salt and pepper. Form mixture into a loaf shape and place in a baking dish. Mix mustard, vinegar, purée, pineapple, sugar and rosemary and rum. Pour this sauce over the loaf. Cook in oven at 180°C (350°F) for 1 1/2 hours, basting regularly. Serve in slices with sauce and baked plantains.

Cinnamon

Cinnamon was monopolised by foreign powers until the 19th century, and until then, the

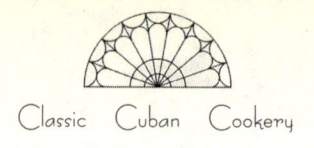

Spanish were forced to make do with Cassia, a slightly inferior alternative, which they imported from China. Cinnamon ('Cinnamomum zeylanicum'), comes from the bark of a 50 foot tree, which is stunted to eight foot when cultivated. The thin bark is stripped from the trunk and dried, to form quills, which are powdered, or used whole. Its Spanish name is 'canela'. Thought to be an aphrodisiac, this ancient spice has an essential oil, which is an astringent and antiseptic. It is used to aid digestion, and in the treatment of stomach disorders.

Cerdo Barbacoa a la Vaguero – Vaguero-Style Barbecued Pork

4 lean, 175g (6oz) pork steaks
1/2 tsp mustard powder
1 tsp fresh root ginger, finely chopped
1/2 tsp ground cinnamon
1/2 tsp dried rosemary
1 tsp allspice
4 tbs corn oil

Mix the spices and herbs together on plate. Rub the mixture into both sides of each steak. Chill the steaks for half an hour. Heat a covered barbecue until grey embers are white hot. Coat the barbecue grill rack with corn oil. Place meat on rack and cover. Cook for half an hour, turning occasionally. Serve sliced, with garlic jucca.

Meat Dishes

Carne Asada - Cuban Roast Beef

900g (2lb) beef steak
2 medium onions, finely sliced
juice of one lime
1 sweet red bell pepper, seeded and chopped
2 garlic cloves, crushed
2 tbs fresh coriander, chopped fine
1/2 tbs olive oil
1/2 tsp dried thyme
1/4 tsp allspice
1/4 tsp black ground pepper
1/2 tsp peppercorns
pinch salt
330ml (12 fl oz) beef stock

Mix lime juice, garlic, coriander, thyme, allspice, pepper. Rub mixture on boths sides of steak, sprinkle with peppercorns. Leave in cool place overnight. Fry onions and sweet pepper in oil until soft. Add the steak, stock, and marinade. Cover and simmer for 1 1/2 hours. Remove beef when tender, and reduce stock to form sauce. Serve beef sliced with sauce and fresh vegetables, rice, or salad.

Hojas de Plátano - Banana Leaves

Banana leaves are used in a variety of ways in the Cuban kitchen. Improvised plates are formed from banana leaves, sieves and small boxes are made from plaited leaf strips. 'Cucurucho' is a sweet made from coconut and sugar is served wrapped in a cone formed from a banana leaf. Banana leaves are also used for cooking large meats, such as a whole suckling pig or pit cooked steaks. The large shiny leaves should be soaked in boiling water for ten minutes to make them supple enough to wrap around the meat. The most common usage of banana leaves is in tamales.

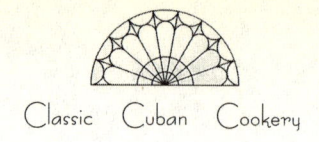

LECHON ASADO – CUBAN STUFFED SUCKLING PIG

6.5kg (15lb) suckling pig, prepared by butcher
6 Habanero chillies, seeded and chopped fine
1 large onion, chopped fine
2 tbs oregano, finely chopped
2 tbs coriander, finely chopped
2 tbs marjoram, finely chopped
3 tbs rosemary, finely chopped
12 garlic cloves, finely chopped
10 juniper berries, stoned and halved
4 tbs salt
2 tbs water
juice of two Cuban oranges

Make a paste of all ingredients except juniper berries and piglet. Gash the carcass with deep cuts all over. Press half the paste mix into the gashes. Mix the other half of the paste with juniper berries. Fill the inside of the carcass with this paste. Leave overnight in a cold place to marinate. Roast in a 180°C (350°F) degree oven, wrapped in foil, for 4 to 5 hours. Baste occasionally, and remove foil. Test that the juices run clear when the meat is pierced. Roast for around half an hour until brown. Wait for quarter of an hour before carving.

Meat Dishes

Cuban Barbecued Pork

4 lean, 175g (6oz) pork steaks
1/2 tsp mustard powder
1 tsp fresh root ginger, finely chopped
1/2 tsp ground cinnamon
1/2 tsp dried rosemary
1 tsp allspice
4 tbs corn oil

Mix the spices and herbs together on plate. Rub the mixture into both sides of each steak. Chill the steaks for half an hour. Heat a covered barbecue until grey embers are white hot. Coat the barbecue grill rack with corn oil. Place meat on rack and cover. Cook for half an hour, turning occasionally. Serve sliced, with garlic jucca. Banana leaves can be used as plates to add authenticity

Bistec en Rollo – Cuban Rolled Beef

Wash hands thoroughly after preparing chillies.

900g (2lb) flank steak
110g (4oz) cooked ham, cut into strips
4 tomatoes, blanched, peeled and chopped
2 crushed garlic cloves
1 peeled carrot, finely sliced
1 large onion, thinly sliced

Classic Cuban Cookery

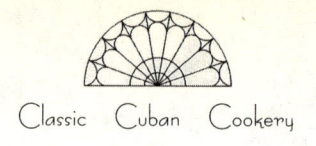

4 tbs lime juice
6 peppercorns
1 tsp soft brown sugar
25g (1oz) ginger root, peeled and finely chopped
1 sweet green bell pepper, chopped
1 Habanero chilli, seeded and finely chopped
25g (1oz) butter, diced small
1 tbs red wine vinegar
125ml red wine
3 tbs palm oil
1 bay leaf
1/2 teaspoon oregano
pinch of salt and pepper

Rub salt, pepper, garlic, and half of the lime juice, into one side of steak. Lay ham strips over the steak. Soak carrot in remaining lime juice for 5 minutes. Sprinkle peppercorns over ham strips. Place drained carrot slices on ham strips. Sprinkle with sugar and diced butter. Roll the steak up tightly and tie with string. Mix wine and vinegar and pour over steak in cooking dish. Let stand for 30 minutes, then take out steak and brown it in oil. Return the steak to the marinade adding rest of ingredients. Cover and simmer for 2 hours. Serve on bed of rice, and pour on the marinade sauce.

In the 1970s, a Cuban couple, Quiqui and Marina, used to entertain their farming friends at their home, just outside Victoria de las Tunas, Las Tunas Province in Southern Cuba. During one of these meals, a motorcycle policeman arrived on the doorstep and announced that Fidel Castro himself would be passing by in a few minutes. Fidel had

Meat Dishes

heard of the couple's hospitality, and had asked to meet them. Quiqui and Marina invited 'El Chef' to join them for lunch. They had prepared a rich stew which they called 'Caldosa'. Fidel was so impressed by this dish that he suggested that they open a restaurant. Restaurant 'Quiqui Marina' still serves Caldosa, made in exactly the same way as served to El Presidente. Caldosa is an aromatic hot pot, with one secret ingredient. Secret, that is, until now.

CALDOSA QUIQUI MARINA – QUIQUI MARINA'S CALDOSA STEW

3.1 kg (3lb) chicken meat, diced3 tbs red beans
110g (4oz) cooked black beans
110g (4oz) frozen peas
225g (8oz) malanga greens, torn into shreds
2 bananas, sliced
900g (2lbs) yucca, chopped into large pieces
175g (6oz) chorizo sausage, chopped roughly
4tbs chopped ham
2 tbs chopped green olives
4 garlic cloves, chopped fine
1 large onion, chopped
1/2 sweet green bell pepper, seeded and chopped
1/2 sweet red bell pepper, seeded and chopped
4 tsp sesame seeds
110 ml (4 fl oz) tomato paste
1 tsp salt
4 tbs peanut butter
2 tbs fresh coriander, finely chopped

Classic Cuban Cookery

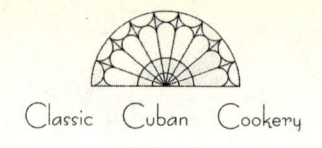

1.75l (3 pints) water
juice of 3 oranges
juice of 2 limes
2 cloves of garlic, crushed
1 small onion, sliced fine
1 tbs white rum
1 tbs sherry
pinch of salt
1/2 tsp mixed herbs
1 tsp dried oregano
1/4 tsp ground cumin
1/2 tsp allspice
1/2 tbs fresh root ginger, finely chopped

Combine the last 12 ingredients into a marinade. Marinate the chicken in the sauce overnight. Drain chicken pieces and brown in oil in deep pan. Remove chicken. Fry onion, sesame seeds, peppers and garlic in oil. Before onions brown, add ham and sausage, cook for 1 minute. Add water, beans, peas, and yucca, cooking for 10 minutes. Stir peanut butter, salt and tomato paste into marinade. Add mixture to the cooking pan. Stir thoroughly. Add malanga greens, coriander, bananas and olives. Stir and simmer for 20 minutes, or until a thick mixture.

Pirates had been using Cuba's Isle of Pines as a base for centuries before Robert Louis Stevenson wrote his book 'Treasure Island', which is based on the large southern island. In 1953, the young revolutionary student, Fidel Castro was held at the prison at the island for his part in the uprising against the Moncada barracks. Today there is an island on the restaurant known as El Conchito, or the Little Pig, which was the Cuban's name for Batista; the dictator who imprisoned Fidel and his comrades. El Conchita serves the best pork dishes on the island, including this simple country dish called Bacan.

BACAN BANANA – BANANAS AND PORK

900g (2lb) minced pork
6 ripe bananas
1 tsp dried rosemary
1 tbs grated coconut meat
pinch of salt and pepper
275 ml (1/2 pint) coconut milk
275ml (1/2 pint) water

Mash together all ingredients except coconut milk and water. Boil mash in milk and water for about 20 minutes, until cooked. Spoon out mixture, serving on banana leaves as plates.

FILETES DE CERDO – PORK FILLETS CUBAN STYLE

900g (2lb) lean pork fillets
3 garlic cloves, crushed
juice of 3 limes
pinch of salt
1/2 tsp chilli powder
55 ml (2 fl oz) olive oil

Mix the garlic, lime juice, salt and chilli in a flat bowl. Marinade the pork in the mixture

Classic Cuban Cookery

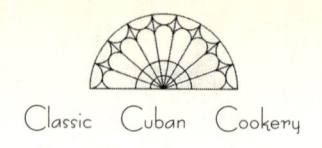

for 2 hours, turning at times. Pour the marinade from the fillets, and scrape them. Heat the oil in a pan and brown both sides of the fillets.

Almost everybody has heard of Sloppy Joe's bar in Key West, but few have heard of the original Sloppy Joe's in Havana. This magnificent neo-classical, colonial style building, standing in Old Havana, was opened in 1917, by the Prohibition-buster, Joe Russell, who was also responsible for the founding of a similar bar in the Florida Keys. From the 1920s until the late 1950s, Havana Sloppy Joe's was a mecca for the rich, the famous and the dubious. In 1959, Graham Greene's novel, 'Our Man in Havana', was made into a film. It starred Sir Alec Guinness and was filmed in the now-defunct bar, but in its heyday, Sloppy Joe's specialised in Planter's Punch, Daiquiris and on their snack menu was their famous inch-thick rye bread, ham and cheese sandwiches and its celebrated picadillo buns, which are a bit like runny hamburgers.

PICADILLO 'SLOPPY JOE'S'

4 onions, peeled and finely chopped
3 garlic cloves, finely chopped
700g (1 1/2 lbs) lean mince
75g (3oz) green olives, stoned and chopped
2 tbs olive oil
75g (3oz) raisins
110 ml (4 fl oz) Gold Rum
2 tbs capers
5 tbs tomato purée
1/2 tbs dried oregano

Meat Dishes

pinch of salt and ground black pepper
four bun rolls, halved

Sauté onions in oil for 10 minutes. Add garlic and meat and brown for around 5 minutes. Reduce the heat and add rum. Add the rest of the ingredients and cook over a low heat for 10 minutes. Stir ingredients and season, stirring well. Spoon cooked mixture into bun rolls.

Churrasco Los Ranchos – Ranch Style Steak

2 350g (12oz) steaks
50g (2oz) chilli powder
1 tbs mixed herbs
2 garlic cloves, crushed
juice of 6 limes
275 ml (1/2 pint) corn oil
75g (3oz) salt
4 sprigs thyme
4 sprigs sage
4 sprigs rosemary
2 sprigs anise
10 bay leaves
2 sprigs fresh coriander

Mix chilli and mixed herbs, cloves, oil, lime juice and salt in a dish. Place steaks in marinade overnight. Heat charcoal barbecue. Grill one side of the steak over barbecue and baste the other side with the marinade. Turn steak over and baste the cooked side with the rest of the marinade. Put bay leaves and sprigs of herbs, except the coriander, directly on coals under the steaks. Burn the sprigs until the steak is done. Serve garnished with coriander sprigs.

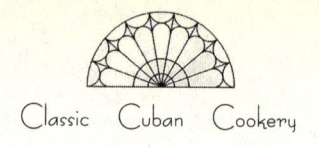

Picadillo Picadura – Cuban Hash

The meat must be marinated overnight.
Wash hands thoroughly after handling chillies

900g (2lb) lean beef, diced
2 large onions, chopped
2 plantains, sliced
6 Habanero chillies, seeded and finely chopped
3 garlic cloves, finely chopped
4 sweet red bell peppers, finely chopped
6 tomatoes, blanched, peeled and chopped
110g (4oz) raisins
6 olives, stoned and halved
2 tbs wine vinegar
1/4 tsp ground cinnamon
1/4 tsp allspice
2 tbs olive oil
250ml pineapple juice
salt and pepper

Cover meat with pineapple juice and leave to stand overnight. Brown meat in oil, saving remaining pineapple juice. Add onions, chillies, garlic, salt, pepper and sauté until soft. Add remaining ingredients, plus pineapple juice. Simmer for about 30 minutes until meat is tender. Serve with jucca boiled with garlic, and rice.

Jackfruit

Jackfruit, or jak fruit ('Artocarpus heterophyllus') is similar to the breadfruit, and can weigh up to 40lbs (20 kilos). They came to the Caribbean from Malaysia, and are a good source of vitamins A and B, containing 12 per cent protein, calcium and carotene. The prickly green fruit has a high starch content and its white, pungent gelatinous flesh is commonly served cooked. The jackfruit, contained in bulbs are tasty when roasted and not unlike chestnuts in flavour.

Jackfruit con Leche de Coco – Jackfruit with Coconut Milk

2 medium jackfruit
450g (1lb) corned pork or beef
cream from large, grated coconuts

Peel breadfruit and cut each into four large wedges. Remove cores. Cut meat into eight slices. Place in a pan under breadfruit and meat. Cover pot and cook until coconut cream has turned to oil.

Calabaza Che – Che-Style Pumpkin with Pork

900 g (2lb) lean pork, diced
1 small pumpkin, peeled and cubed

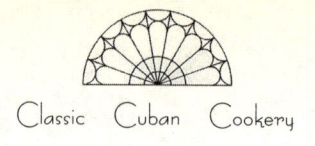

1 sweet potato, peeled and sliced
1 yam, peeled and sliced
2 medium onions, peeled and chopped
1 sweet red bell pepper, chopped
2 tomatoes, blanched, peeled and chopped
2 plantains, peeled and sliced
4 Habanero chillies, seeded and chopped fine
3 garlic cloves, chopped fine
3 tbs olive oil
juice of 2 limes
800ml (1 1/2 pints) water
salt and pepper

Bring pork to boil in water, Cover and simmer for 45 minutes. Add pumpkin, sweet potato, yam, and simmer for 15 minutes. In separate pan, sauté onions, pepper, chilli and garlic in oil. Pour mixture over the pork and vegetables. Add tomato and bananas. Simmer for around 20 minutes, until vegetables are tender. Stir in lime juice. Season with salt and pepper.

Squash

Squashes, or gourds, have grown in Cuba since Arawak times. The dried shells were used as cups, bowls and dishes. The Amerindians would use gourd shells to catch wildfowl by floating empty shells on the water when a flock of birds landed on it. The hunter would then place half a gourd on his head and approach the birds, while using a reed as a breathing tube. Once near enough, the hunter would pull the bird under the water by grabbing its legs.

Meat Dishes

Calabaza con Cerdo – Pumpkin and Pork

    900g (2lb) lean pork, diced
    1 small pumpkin, peeled and cubed
    1 sweet potato, peeled and sliced
    1 yam, peeled and sliced
    2 medium onions, peeled and chopped
    1 sweet red bell pepper, chopped
    2 tomatoes, blanched, peeled and chopped
    2 plantains, peeled and sliced
    4 Habanero chillies, seeded and chopped fine
    3 garlic cloves, chopped fine
    3 tablespoons olive oil
    juice of 2 limes
    1 1/2 pint water
    salt and pepper

Bring pork to boil in water, Cover and simmer for 45 minutes. Add pumpkin, sweet potato, yam, and simmer for 15 minutes. In separate pan, sauté onions, pepper, chilli and garlic in oil. Pour mixture over the pork and vegetables. Add tomato and bananas. Simmer for around 20 minutes, until vegetables are tender. Stir in juice of limes. Season with salt and pepper.

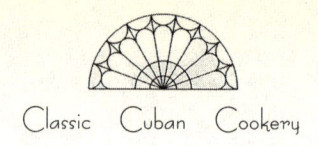

Olives

Early settlers in Cuba were forbidden to grow olives in the New World on orders of the Monarchy, so that the livelihoods of the Spanish traders was not endangered. Initially, olive oil was shipped to Cuba in barrels, but later the tinajon, a clay vessel was used instead. Olive oil is an essential ingredient in Cuban cookery, used neat on salads and in sauces. Olives are also added whole in some recipes. The American oil palm yields an oil that is an effective substitute to olive oil in terms of its composition, appearance and quality.

Pimentio Disecado Chorizo – Rice Stuffed Peppers

   4 large sweet green or red bell peppers
   225g (8oz) Chorizo sausage meat, chopped
   1 small onion, chopped fine
   1 clove garlic, crushed
   450g (1lb) tomatoes, skinned and chopped
   150g (5oz) cooked long grain rice
   1 tsp coriander seeds
   1 tbs fresh coriander, chopped
   1 tsp salt
   1/2 tsp ground black pepper
   1 1/2 tbs olive oil

Cook tomatoes until soft. Slice 1 cm from the pepper and scoop out the pith and seeds. Fry onions and garlic in 1 tbs of oil until soft. Add sausage meat and cook, stirring frequently for 6 minutes. Add the rest of the ingredients except for the rice. Simmer for 30 minutes.

Add rice and cook for 5 minutes. Fill mixture into each upright pepper and replace top. Bake for around 40 minutes in a fairly hot oven.

Albondigas Bayamese – Cuban Meatballs in a Hot Sauce

   900g (2lbs) minced pork or beef, or half of each
   3 garlic cloves, finely chopped
   50g (2oz) fresh breadcrumbs
   1 egg
   1/2 tsp allspice
   1/2 dried rosemary
   25g (1oz) root ginger, peeled finely chopped
   25ml (1 fl oz) Gold rum
   4 tbs maize flour
   6 tbs maize oil

Mix all ingredients except 2 tablespoons of flour and the oil. Sprinkle 2 tablespoons of flour onto a cooking board. Shape mixture into about 15 balls and roll in the flour to coat them. Heat the oil in the pan and fry the balls until brown all over. Serve on a bed of rice with Salsa Habanero, and garlic jucca.

Estofado Con Pollo Y Calabacita – Chicken and Pumpkin Stew

   900g (2lbs) chicken meat, cut into bite-size pieces
   1.2 kg (2 1/2 lb) pumpkin, or squash flesh, diced

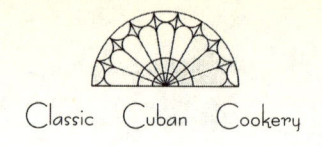

1 large onion, chopped
2 sweet green bell peppers, seeded and chopped
2 Poblano chillies, seeded and copped fine
1 aubergine, peeled and cubed
150g (5oz) peanut butter
1 tsp salt
4 tbs sunflower oil
250ml (8 fl oz) boiling water

Heat oil in large pot. Brown chicken in the oil, and then add onions and peppers. Dissolve peanut butter in hot water. Stir peanut water into chicken mix. Add salt, aubergine, and pumpkin. Cover pot and simmer all ingredients for 50 minutes. Serve with rice.

Arroz con Pollo Santiago – Santiago Chicken and Rice

This is the combination of two recipes - one for the rice and one for the chicken.

Sauce:
6 Jalapeno chilli peppers, finely chopped
110g (4oz) papaya flesh, finely chopped
2 large onions, finely chopped
3 cloves of garlic, finely chopped
25g (1oz) root ginger, peeled and finely chopped
1/2 tsp turmeric
3 tbs malt vinegar
dash of Tabasco sauce

Meat Dishes

dash of Worcestershire sauce
1 tsp salt
1/2 tsp pepper
1 tsp brown sugar

Add all the ingredients to a pan and bring to the boil. Reduce the heat and simmer for 5 minutes, stirring constantly. Blend or purée until smooth.

Chicken:
900g (2lb) chicken, cut into portions
2 sweet red bell peppers, finely chopped
1 large onion, peeled and quartered
110g (4oz) canned peas
4tbs olive oil
1.2 l (2 pints) chicken stock
225g (8oz) rice

Fry onion quarter and bell peppers until soft. Set aside. Pour smooth sauce over chicken quarters in dish. Stand for 4 hours. Clean the chicken from the marinade, reserving sauce. Lightly brown chicken pieces in the oil. Remove chicken from pan and sauté rice in pan until light brown. Turn rice into casserole dish, add the sauce. Add peas, cooked peppers, onion, stock and chicken. Cover and cook for 30 minutes, or until rice and chicken are done.

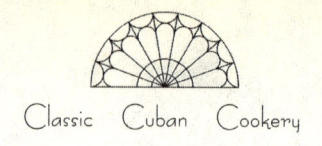

Pato Platano – Roast Duck with Chorizo and Orange Stuffing

2.25kg (5lb) whole duck
450g (1lb) chorizo sausage, sliced thick
1 large onion, chopped
1 slice stale bread, crumbled
1 tbs maize oil
1 tbs milk
4 plátano bananas, mashed
1/2 tsp dried sage
1/2 tsp salt
1/2 tsp ground black pepper
4 tbs milk
juice of 3 large oranges

Cook onion in oil until golden. Tear the sausage slices into pieces and add to onions. Cook for around 3 minutes. Add crumbled bread, milk, sage, salt and pepper. Simmer, stirring frequently for 20 minutes. In a pan, simmer plantains in orange juice until mushy, Add plantains to sausage mixture. Stir and cook for 3 minutes. Stuff duck with mixture. Truss and place on roasting dish. Cook in oven at 180°C 350°F for around 2 hours, basting regularly.

Meat Dishes

Sesame

The sesame plant ('Sesamum indicum') originated in Africa and was brought to Cuba by West African slaves who valued the high oil content of the seed, which could be used as a cooking oil. The creamy coloured seeds are used in baking to flavour breads and pastries and are also used in stews and soups. Sesame seeds fried in butter make an interesting dressing for salads and they can be used as a substitute for nuts because of their flavour.

CALDILLO CUBANO – CUBAN HOTPOT

900g (2lbs) braising steak, cubed
2 large onions, chopped
2 large tomatoes, chopped
4 sweet potatoes, chopped
1 large potato chopped
8 Jalapeno chillies, seeded and finely chopped
2 garlic cloves, chopped fine
1 tsp brown soft sugar
1/4 tsp cumin seeds
2 tbs corn oil
1.2 l (2 pints) water

Brown meat in the oil, adding garlic and onions. Sauté for ten minutes. Mix all the other ingredients in casarole dish. Cover with water. Add meat, onions and garlic. Cook for around two hours, until meat is very tender.

Classic Cuban Cookery

Classic Cuban Cookery

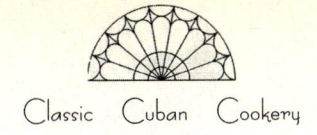

Sauces

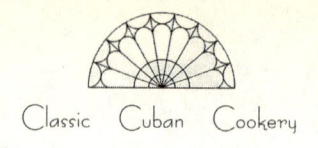

Marina Hemingway, Santa Fe

Santa Fe district is a short distance west of Havana, and it boasts a first class marina resort. Built in the 1950s as a yacht and fishing club, the Hemingway Marina offers berthing space for over 400 ocean-going yachts and fishing boats. 'El Viejo y El Mar' apartment hotel in the marina, and the 'Villa Paraíso' apartments and bungalows both offer extensive accommodation. Duty-free shops, a supermarket and 'La Vigía' shopping centre, are on site, as are the seafood restaurants 'Papa's', the companion restaurant 'Fiesta', named after another of Hemingway's books and the 'Rincón de Mexico', which serves typical Mexican cuisine. There is also the 'Los Paraguitas' cafeteria and hotel's complex of bars and its 'Cojímar' restaurant.

The scaffolding on the waterside near 'Papas' restaurant is not for hanging pirates; it is used to weigh the giant marlin that are caught during the Currican fishing tournament, held during the last two weeks of April. In 1951, the Ernest Hemingway fishing tournament was established and, in May 1960, the winner of the trophy was Fidel Castro himself. The Marina Hemingway, named after the Nobel Prize-winning author, is a duty-free area, dubbed 'An Island in the Gulf'.

Sauces

The word salsa is the Cuban term for sauce that has been used for many years. However, salsa was used to describe a style of music in 1928 - local musicians had a tendency to pep up the languid and romantic popular tunes of the day, and Ignacio Pineiro penned the song 'Echale Salsita', translated as 'put a little sauce into it!'

In 1970, a New York record company adopted the word salsa to describe the sound that their Cuban groups were creating, and today salsa is synonymous with the beat of Cuba's distinct rhythm.

On the culinary side, Cuba's chefs produce a wide variety of salsas, from the mild

Sauces

cucumber sauces to the fiery habanero salsa, one of the hottest sauces known and rivalling the hot tabasco-style sauces. Generally, the more creole the dish, the hotter the salsa.

The main ingredient of Cuba's sauces is normally chilli, but they also include herbs and spices from all over the world. Spain's influence is found in the sofrito, which is a preparation of garlic and onions, which in itself forms the basis for many salsas.

Sauces are used for a variety of functions - for dipping, for tapas, snacks and side dishes - they are so much more than a covering for the main dish. Some salsas are even used as the base for soups and stews. Normally a salsa will be provided alongside a dish, so the diner can add the sauce to taste - beware - many of them are very hot!

The History of Caribbean Chillies and Peppers

The chilli plant ('Capsicum frutescens') was one of Spain's most rewarding discoveries on Columbus' second voyage to the New World between 1493-96. Up until then, most spices, including pepper were obtained through the long and expensive trade route to Asia. The peppercorn is native to India, but both hot chillies and sweet peppers are indigenous to the Americas.

The aim of Columbus' journey was to find a fast sea passage from Europe to the East Indies for trade purposes, but instead he stumbled on the New World in 1492, discovering a whole range of chillies and peppers on the way.

Columbus' small band of explorers noted the use of chilli by the Arawaks. The local Amerindian's staple diet was cassava, a starchy root tuber. Chilli was added to the cassava to add flavour and also aid digestion by the Mexican Aztecs, the Maya of Central America, the Incas of Peru long before the arrival of the first Europeans. It is known that chillies have been part of the indigenous diet since 5000BC, enhancing the plentiful fish and shellfish around the Caribbean coastline.

Columbus was anxious to please the Spanish monarchs, who had authorised and *subsidised his first voyage, and so he took as many samples of the vegetation as possible back to Spain, believing that he had found the eastern coast of Asia. That he had not even found one of the familiar Asian foodstuffs in the Caribbean, should have alerted Columbus to the fact that he had found a completely new world.*

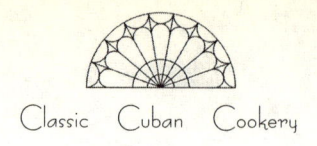

The early colonists learned several skills from the indigenous Arawaks, including the art of preserving meats with natural herbs and spices. This involved barbecuing meats that had been infused with local peppers and chillies and then wrapped in banana leaves before cooking. Itinerant livestock traders or buccaneers, used the Arawak barbecue to smoke the meat, which would keep longer than salted meats. These buccaneers, mostly outlaws, lived by preying on herds of wild cattle and pigs.

Up until the mid-16th century, mariners survived the long transatlantic journeys by living off salted meat. However, such meat had to be washed using the ship's precious supply of fresh water before it was palatable. Essential for preserving food, the buccaneers found the chilli pepper a fine alternative to the black pepper ('piper nigrum'). It is ideal for preserving meat as it contains an antibacterial agent and is also rich in vitamin C.

This process is still used in Cuba and Jamaica today, where the meat is known as jerked pork or beef jerky. The word jerk came from the Latin American Spanish for sun-dried, charquear, and the Peruvian Inca tribe's Quechua word, echarqui. This type of dried meat is also known as cecina.

By the early 1500s, Europeans discovered the curative properties of chilli. They used cayenne pepper powder to make poultices to treat muscular aches and pains and cure colds and circulatory disorders, and they used peppers to treat kidney and stomach ailments.

Sauces

Chillies and Peppers

Today, chillies and capsicum peppers are integral ingredients in Cuban cuisine. There are two main varieties of chilli, from the fiery hot peppers to the sweet mild capsicum, and both are the native to the Americas. Capsicum means 'little case' in Latin, and is so named because both chillies and sweet peppers are hollow and contain a fleshy core surrounded by many tiny seeds. The skin of both peppers and chillies are tough and thin, and the flesh of the pepper is generally thicker than that of the chilli. The Sweet, Capsicum, Bullnose, Pimento, Paprika or Bell pepper (all names for the same plant) grows to only half the height of the chilli plant, which can reach 2 metres. Both chillies and peppers belong to the Solanaceae family, which includes the tomato, potato and nightshade plants. Chillies can be a variety of colours, including yellow, orange, green and red, and peppers can in addition be white or purple.
Chillies are grown in the tropics from sea level up to an altitude of 2000m, and both chillies and peppers will grow in more temperate climates during the summer.
There are now more than 1,600 varieties of chilli grown world wide, of which there are around 100 local varieties in the Caribbean. Capsicums are widely cultivated throughout the world. Chillies and peppers have little food value, containing about 38 calories per 100 grams. They are also rich in vitamins A and C and contain antibacterial properties.

Going for the Burn

Everyone remembers their first encounter with a chilli. Almost without exception, the primary memory is one of heat and the burn of the pepper. Curiously, the pain of a chilli is somehow comfortable, but it can be extreme enough to cause almost unbearable pain. Capsaicin, the essential oil in chilli is responsible for the burning heat of chillies and also increases the circulation and blood pressure. It is found in the skin, seeds and veins of the fruit, and when eaten, it causes the body to release endorphins, which are natural opiates, so promoting a feeling of well-being. These endorphins are also a natural analgesic. After eating a chilli, the tear ducts are automatically stimulated, as are the perspiration glands in the skin, along with the mucous membranes in the nose and elsewhere. Chilli can burn the eyes and skin on contact, and so it is very important to wash one's hands after handling chilli - some people prefer to wear gloves when using it in the kitchen. If your mouth feels like its on fire after indulging in chilli, do not drink water, because it will only exacerbate the sensation. Instead, eat bread, plain rice or better still, dairy produce such as cheese and yoghurt, as capsaicin is soluble in fat and not water.

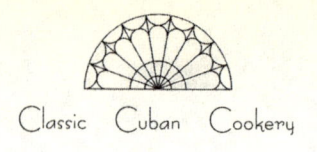

A Chilli Compendium

Capsaicin is measured in scientific units called Scovilles, literally the Richter scale of the vegetable world. The Scoville scale ranges from the mildest, the bell pepper, classified as 0, to the hottest, the Habanero, which is estimated at a staggering 300,000! However, for ease, most cooks rate the capsaicin content of chillies in units from 0 to 100.

HABANERO CHILLI - This small lantern shaped chilli can be orange-red, green or yellow, and is the hottest known chilli. It is named after the city of Havana, and its passionate and racy inhabitants. It scores 100 on the Scoville scale.

BIRD'S EYE CHILLI (REDCAP CHILLI) - This oval, bright orange chilli is generally about 2 centimetres long and when cut, it exudes an aroma similar to freshly sliced melon. It rates around 90 on the Scoville scale.

DE ARBOL CHILLI - the long and thin, pointed red De Arbol chilli rates at 80 on the Scoville scale.

Sauces

Piquin (or Flea) Chilli - this is as hot as the de Arbol. This chilli is tiny and oval, with a nutty taste. These are usually used in sauces, and to flavour oils and vinegars. The fiery hot Tepin chilli is also said to taste of nuts and corn. The Piquin scores 80 on the Scoville scale.

Jalapeno Chilli - As a rule, fleshy chillies such as this one are less hot than those with less flesh. The jalapeno is dark green and very fleshy, growing to about 5 centimetres. It scores 60 on the Scoville scale. The smoked jalapeno is known as the Chipotle, which has a nutty and smoky flavour.

Serrano Chilli - The small bright green serrano chilli is often pickled and is known in Spanish as 'en escabeche' It is widely used in cooking and it is about 4 centimetres in length, round and quite hot, scoring 50 on the Scoville scale.

Costerno Amarillo - this is a yellow pepper with a delicate lime flavour and is moderate in heat, with 40 Scoville points.

Amaheim (Californian) Chilli - this is either red or green and is one of the most commonly used chillies. It is 40 on the scale.

Pasilla Chilli - the pasilla is long, thin and dark, and an excellent addition to seafood. Its name means 'little raisin' for its looks and this mild chilli tastes of berries and liquorice. It rates about 40 on the heat scale.

Cascabel Chilli - the name of this chilli translates to 'little rattle'. Its thick flesh has a nutty flavour and is mainly used in sauces, stews and soups. 40 Scoville points.

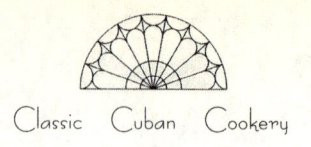

Poblano (Ancho) Chilli - a chocolate coloured chilli, which when dried is known as the Ancho. These chillies are large enough to be stuffed, but they are also used in sauces. The chillies have a very thin dark brown skin and are very fleshy. The fresh chilli is 40 on the scale, but once dried are only 30. Other chillies similar to the ancho are the romesco and mulato chillies.

Guajillo Chilli - this mild and brightly coloured chilli is used to colour dishes and impart a delightful warm heat. It is said that the flavour of this chilli resembles that of fresh green tea. It scores 30 on the Scoville scale.

Pasado Chilli - this is often roasted and it acquires a fruity taste which is suited to soups and stews, and it also has 30 points. Other chillies with 30 points are the Chilli Seco, the Guindilla, Caribe and Morron chillies.

Nora Chilli - this is a very mild chilli and is sweet and fruity and mostly used in soups and stews. It only has between 10 and 20 Scoville points, as does the Choricero, which are used in the chorizo pepper.

Cooking with Chillies and Peppers

There are three distinct methods of cooking with chillies, whereby the heat of a dish can be controlled. Firstly, to gain the flavour of the chilli without the heat, cook with whole chillies and then discard them after cooking. To add a moderate heat, halve the chillies, remove the pith and seeds and add them to the dish. To get full heat and flavour, chop the chillies, along with the pith and seeds into the dish.
Always taste the dish for heat as it is cooking. Should the dish prove too hot, a little sugar tends to temper the heat of the chilli.

Some cooks like to skin peppers which are to be stuffed, such as the poblano, pasilla, mulato or capsicum. It is easier to skin them if they are first grilled or charred. The peppers or chillies should be placed under a hot grill until they blister. This also gives the peppers a smoky flavour and a sweet juicy texture.

Cayenne Pepper

Many varieties of chilli, including the very hot cayenne chilli are dried, ground and blended to make cayenne pepper. Sometimes other spices and seeds as well as salt are added to the powder, and a cayenne sauce can be made in the same way but with the addition of vinegar.

Achiote Powder

A mixture of ground spices, herbs, chillies and achiote or annatto combine to form this powder, which adds colour and pungency to a variety of dishes. This powder is often mixed with lime juice and olive oil to make a marinade for fish and meat before barbecuing or grilling. Achiote can come in paste or block form, when it is dissolved in grapefruit juice before using. Achiote is used to flavour fish, poultry or meat. The orange-red seed of the Bixa tree is known as 'annatto', and have a covering which produces a red or yellow vegetable dye, used for colouring foods and giving olive oil an orange tint.

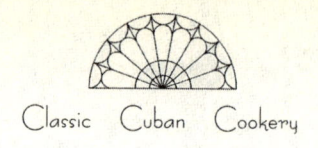

Havana Ancho Adobo – Havana Pickle Sauce

This pickle or sauce is ideal as a dip or to enhance the flavour of soups or stews.

- 12 dried Ancho chillies, sliced lengthways
- 1 fresh Habanero chilli, quartered
- 2 medium onions, finely sliced
- 6 garlic cloves, finely sliced
- 4 tbs tomato ketchup
- 1 tbs tomato purée
- 5 tbs vinegar
- 1 tsp salt
- 750ml (1.25 pints) water

Simmer all ingredients gently in the water for approximately 50 minutes. Blend into a paste, which can be used as a pickle, sauce or food enhancement.

Annatto

Annatto, or achiote, is the name for the orange-red seeds of a native New World tree, ('Bixa orellana'). The 15 foot (4.5 metre) high tree is indigenous to Cuba, and is an evergreen. This tree produces a 2-inch wide capsule, covered in soft spines. Inside the capsule, are 20 to 50 seeds, rich in vitamin A. It is the covering of these seeds which yield a red or yellow, vegetable dye, when boiled. The seeds lend a rich colour to the oil in which they are cooked, and the coloured oil is often added to Cuban sauces, and also used for cooking. The Arawaks painted the dye on their faces, as it acts as a sun screen, and an insect repellent. The following peanut sauce is cooked in annatto-coloured oil.

Sauces

SALSA DE MANI – PEANUT SAUCE

2 tbs annatto seeds
2 tbs groundnut oil
1 medium onion, chopped fine
2 cloves of garlic, chopped fine
2 tomatoes, blanched, peeled, seeded and chopped
4 tbs smooth peanut butter
pinch of salt.

Heat annatto seeds in oil for 1 minute. Discard seeds. Bring oil back up to heat and cook onions in it until tender. Add garlic and sauté for a few minutes. Stir in tomatoes, blending over heat for 10 minutes. Blend in peanut butter, and season with salt.

PIQUIN Y MANI SALSA – PIQUIN CHILLI AND PEANUT SAUCE

The hot piquin chillies are toned down by peanut butter.

10 Piquin chillies, seeded and finely chopped
1 large onion, finely chopped
4 cloves garlic, finely chopped
3 large tomatoes, chopped
6 tbs peanut butter
2 tsp lime juice
50g (2oz) butter
125ml (4 fl oz) coconut milk

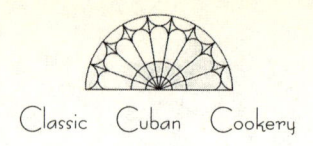

Sauté the onion and garlic in butter. Add tomatoes, chillies and peanut butter. Stir whilst cooking for 5 minutes. Pour mixture into the blender and add lime juice. Blend, adjusting the consistency with coconut milk.

Mantequilla de Mani – Peanut Butter

    450g (1lb) shelled, skinned, roasted peanuts
    55ml (2 fl oz) peanut oil
    1 tsp salt
    1 Jalapeno chilli, seeded and finely chopped

Blend the nuts and chilli in an electric blender for just under 1 minute. Crunchier peanut butter can be made by reducing the blending time. Mix the ground nuts, oil and salt together in a bowl. Preserve peanut butter in a screw top jar.

Salsa Borracha – 'Drunken' Sauce

    6 Ancho chillies, chopped
    1/4 bottle Cuban Gold rum
    2 tomatoes, peeled and chopped
    1 small onion, finely chopped
    1 clove garlic
    1/2 tsp salt
    1/4 tsp brown sugar
    1 tbs olive oil

Sauces

Soak the chillies in the rum overnight. Purée all ingredients, except oil in a blender. Add the mixture to hot oil in a pan. Fry, stirring occasionally, for 5 minutes.

Avocado

The avocado ('Persea americana'), or aguacate is a fruit which is treated more like a vegetable in the Cuban kitchen. This native fruit arrived in Cuba from Mexico, brought by the Spanish conquistador, Encisco, who distributed it throughout the Caribbean. The avocado pear varies in size, and can be oval or round - there are about 400 varieties of the fruit. A native to Central America, the avocado can reach 300 grams and can be dark green or purple in colour.
Rich in vitamins A, B, E, and a range of minerals, the avocado is high in calories, and it contains virtually no carbohydrate, but has a rare, easily digestible oil, being up to 25 per cent fat. The fruit is soft and creamy when ripe and matures all year round. Its delicate flesh is used in salads, soups, sauces and as a dessert, but it has a tendency to discolour quickly. To prevent this, squeeze lime or lemon juice on the flesh. Avacado slasa makes an excellent side salad, a sauce for barbecues, or a dip.

AGUACATE SALSA - AVOCADO SAUCE

1 large avocado, seeded, peeled, and diced
1 sweet red bell pepper, seeded and chopped
1 peeled cucumber, seeded and chopped
450g (1lb) peeled, seeded tomatoes, chopped
1 medium onion, peeled and chopped fine
1 tbs white rum

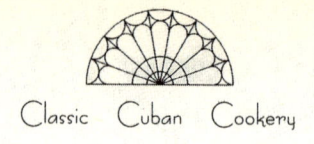

1 tbs brown sugar
1/2 tsp cumin seeds
1/4 tsp ground ginger
juice of half a lime
1/4 tsp salt

Mix all ingredients together thoroughly in a large bowl.

Salsa Marinero – Cuban Seafood Sauce

2 fresh Serrano chillies, seeded, and chopped fine
1 medium onion, finely chopped
1 garlic cloves, chopped fine
2 drops Tabasco sauce
juice of 2 limes
25g (1oz) butter
1/2 tsp cumin powder
pinch of salt

Marinate onions in lime juice for 1 hour. Drain onions and save juice. Fry the onions in butter until soft. Add rest of ingredients and cook slowly for 15 minutes.

Sauces

Tomaton

Originating in Latin America, and grown in parts of Cuba, the Tomaton is a yellow, cherry-like fruit which matures all the year round in a papery pod. The Tomaton is native to the area. Its red-skinned, oval fruit, is eaten raw or made into a jam. The inside is rather like a tomato and this fruit can grow to 120 grams.

TOMATILLO SALSA – TOMATON SAUCE

225g (8oz) tomaton flesh, simmered for 10 minutes
2 Serrano chillies
1/2 onion
2 tbs fresh coriander leaves
1 garlic clove, peeled
1/4 tsp salt
1/4 tsp sugar
3 tbs water

Chop all ingredients roughly in a food mixer, except water. Beat in the water. Place in fridge to cool. Serve with meat dishes.

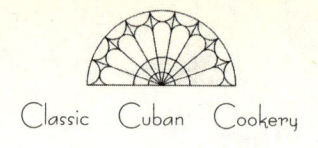

Red Chilli Sauce

Remember to wash hands thoroughly after handling chillies.

    6 fresh Jalapeno chillies, seeded, and chopped fine
    450g (1lb) tomatoes, blanched, seeded, skinned, and chopped small
    1 medium onion, finely chopped
    2 garlic cloves, chopped fine
    1 tsp ground coriander
    2 tbs brown sugar
    1 tbs wine vinegar
    4 tbs tomato ketchup
    2 fluid ounces of maize oil
    4 tbs water

Fry onions and garlic in oil until soft. Purée chillies and tomatoes with the water. Add the onions and the rest of ingredients, and purée. Simmer the mixture for 10 minutes, and let cool. Purée mixture again, and serve.

Salsa de Chilli Verde

This sauce can be served with meat or fish.

    6 fresh thin, green chillies, seeded, and chopped fine
    1 tomato, blanched, skinned, and chopped small
    1 large onion, finely chopped

Sauces

    2 garlic cloves, chopped fine
    1 tsp ground chilli
    1/2 tsp ground coriander
    1/2 tsp ground cumin
    2 tbs maize oil
    330 ml (12 fl oz) water
    pinch of salt

Fry onions and garlic in oil until soft. Add remaining ingredients and simmer for 30 minutes. Let cool and blend to a purée.

Pepino Salsa – Cucumber Salsa

    1 large cucumber sliced roughly
    10g (1/2oz) fresh mint, chopped finely
    2 garlic cloves, peeled and chopped
    1/2 tsp fresh ground black pepper
    1/4 tsp salt
    1/2 tsp vinegar
    2 limes, chopped

Blend all ingredients, except cucumber, into a smooth paste. Add cucumber to the paste, and stop blender when chopped small. Chill salsa before serving.

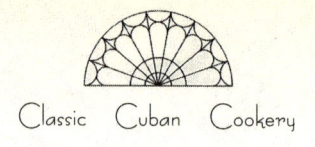

Mango Chutney

4 large mangoes, peeled and stoned
12 garlic cloves, finely chopped
1 sweet red bell pepper, seeded and chopped fine
110g (4oz) raisins
110g (4oz) stoned dates, chopped
1 stick cinnamon, powdered
1 teaspoon allspice
110g (4oz) root ginger, peeled and finely chopped
450g (1lb) granulated sugar
2 tsp chilli powder
2 Jalapeno chillies, chopped fine
4 tbs salt
570ml (1 pint) malt vinegar
1.7 l (3 pints) water

Dissolve salt in the water, dice mango flesh, and add to the water. Leave to stand overnight. Dissolve the sugar in the vinegar over heat, stirring, then boil. Add drained mangoes, ginger, garlic, chilli, raisins, and dates. Stir in the cinnamon, chillies, sweet pepper, and allspice. Bring to boil whilst stirring mixture. Reduce to simmer for 1 to 2 hours, stirring occasionally. Take off heat when mixture is thick. Bottle in preserving jars and seal.

Chillies are also used medicinally, as a stimulant, an aid to digestion, and to produce warmth. Tabasco Sauce, named after a place and river in Mexico, is made from the pickled flesh of chillies, and can be extremely hot, coming in a variety of forms, Habanero Sauce being the hottest one, made from the singularly hot chilli. This last sauce is sometimes made with just the Habanero chilli, salt, and vinegar. This would be used to preserve and pickle meats. However a more widely used preparation includes onions, spices, annatto oil, vinegar, salt, sugar, red wine, sherry, tomatoes, and Habanero chillies.

SALSA HABANERO

This incredibly hot sauce can be further enhanced by adding more Tabasco.

6 fresh Habanero chillies, seeded, and finely chopped
110g (4oz) papaya, finely chopped
3 medium onions, finely chopped
3 garlic cloves, chopped fine
1/2 tsp turmeric
3 tbs malt vinegar
1 tsp salt
1 tsp Tabasco sauce
1/4 tsp allspice
1 tsp annatto flavoured oil
1 tsp brown sugar
1 tbs red wine
1 tbs sherry
1 tbs tomato purée
1 tbs Anejo rum

Bring to boil all ingredients in a saucepan, stirring constantly. Reduce heat and simmer for 5 minutes. Let sauce cool, and blend to a smooth purée.

Classic Cuban Cookery

Classic Cuban Cookery

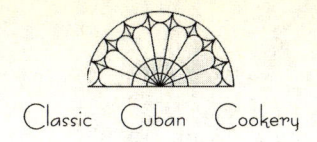

Seafood Dishes

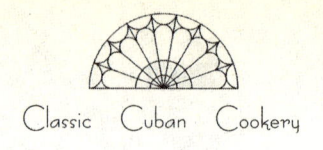

El Floridita Restaurant, Havana

If you are visiting Cuba, then a visit to the Floridita restaurant is a must. Located at 353 Avenida Belgica, the Floridita was where Hemigway sipped his Daiquiris, which is the reason that this famous restaurant is known as the 'cradle of the Daiquiri'. It was here that the famous writer set the record for the number of 'Papa Dobles' drunk in one session; Hemingway managed fourteen in an evening. The barman, Constante had a repertoire of 150 cocktail recipes, and he was immortalised and celebrated in Esquire's 1953 'Famous Bars' article.

The elegant colonial decor is highlighted by the 40 foot mahogany bar, one corner of which is devoted to Hemingway memorabilia. A bust of the author is placed in what was his favourite seat at the bar. La Floridita also serves some of the best lobster in the Caribbean, and Moros y Christianos (Moors and Christians), a mixture of black beans and rice, is just one of the Cuban speciaities served here. In 1820, the 'La Pina del Plata' restaurant was built on this site. Now known as the Floridita, the site has been expanded to include La Pina del Plata ber, the Casa del Tobaco and the Casa del Ron.

Seafood dishes

Cuba's three seas are rich in crustaceans and molluscs. Many stretches of coast are blanketed by mangrove roots, which are a haven for many fish and are the source of ostiones - a small, sweet edible mussel. The island's many coral reefs are home to the edible conch. Other delicacies from the sea include crabs, langosta - the Caribbean lobster - and crayfish, prawns and shrimp. Usually, when seafood is served in Cuba, it is accompanied by a small dish of the ubiquitous sauce known as 'mojito'. Not to be confused with the mojito cocktail, the word mojito comes from the Spanish for a garlic sauce, the 'mojo'. The mojito is often used as a marinade for both fish dishes and meats.

Seafood Dishes

MOJITO SAUCE AND MARINADE

2 large Spanish onions, very finely chopped
6 garlic cloves, crushed
1 tbs fresh root ginger, grated
juice of 10 oranges
juice of 5 limes
2 tbs gold rum
1 tsp ground cumin
2 tsp dried oregano
2 tsp salt
2 tsp honey

Mix the fruit juices together and stir in the olive oil. Add the rest of the ingredients and stir thoroughly. Marinate fish or meat in these juices.

Conch

The Conch, pronounced 'Conk' in English, is known as 'concha' in Spanish, and is synonymous with the Caribbean. One of the largest molluscs in the sea, the conch is part of the Strombus family, which includes the beautiful orange-lined and chocolate-lipped Queen Conch and the Strombus gigas, which is most commonly used in soups and stews. The knobbly golden shell of the conch is a delicate porcelain pink inside and the flared pale pink lip protects the sea snail's delicate flesh. Arawak Amerindians on Cuba once used the conch shell as a primitive trumpet and the meat formed an important part of their diet. Today, conch chowder is an exceptional delicacy, and the meat also makes an excellent salad base.

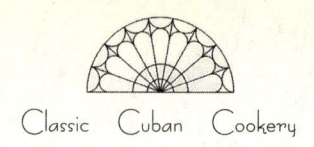

Arawak Ensalada Concha – Cuban-Style Conch Salad

>450g (1lb) conch meat, cut into dice-size chunks
>1 medium onion, chopped
>2 celery stalks, chopped
>1 half-ripe tomato
>1 sweet green bell pepper, seeded and chopped
>1 scotch bonnet chilli, seeded and chopped fine
>1 tsp salt
>8 tbs lime juice
>6 tbs orange juice
>2 mint leaves, finely chopped
>jícama root, grated
>slice of lime
>sprig of mint

Marinade the conch chunks in the lime juice for 2 hours. Mix all the other ingredients, except orange juice, in a bowl. Scatter in conch chunks, and pour over lime and orange juice. Sprinkle chopped mint and grated jícama on salad. Garnish with mint sprig and lime slice

Congrejo Fruta Bomba – Crab with Papaya

>450g (1lb) white crab meat
>3 fresh ripe papayas, skinned and seeded
>1 large shallot, peeled and sliced fine

Seafood Dishes

4 ripe tomatoes, peeled and seeded
half sweet red bell pepper, seeded and diced
1 Serrano chilli, seeded and chopped fine
1/2 tsp fresh ginger, chopped fine
1 tbs fresh coriander, finely chopped
juice of 1 lime
pinch salt and black ground pepper
cleaned shells of four medium-sized crabs

Dice the papaya flesh into very small squares. Mix papaya with shallot and cover with lime juice. Sprinkle over with salt and pepper. Dice the tomatoes in the same way as the papaya. Add tomato, bell pepper, chilli, and ginger to the mix. Mix all ingredients together and spoon into crab shells. Divide the crab meat and spoon onto the mixture in the shells. Sprinkle with the coriander. Place in refrigerator for 1 hour before serving.

In 1946, Frank Sinatra flew into Havana to sing at the Hotel Nacional's nightclub, the 'Cabaret Parisien'. When he arrived at the hotel, Sinatra found a week-long party in progress. He was immediately ushered into the hotel's plush Aguiar Restaurant by Meyer Lansky and 'Lucky' Luciano, who had hired him to sing there. The three sat down to their favourite meal of stone crabs, just one of the ingredients in this next Cuban speciality.

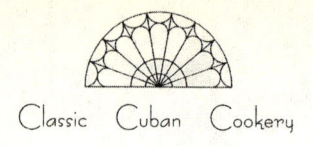

CRIOLLO STONE CRABS

Wash hands thoroughly after chopping chilli peppers.

450g (1lb) crab meat, taken from the crab shells and cooked
empty shells of the stone crabs
6 small green chilli peppers, finely chopped
1/2 sweet red bell pepper finely chopped
2 tomatoes, blanched peeled and finely chopped
2 large onions, finely chopped
50g (2oz) root ginger, peeled and finely chopped
2 cloves garlic, finely chopped
2 tbs tomato purée
2 tbs olive oil
25g (1oz) grated coconut
3 tbs gold rum
juice of 3 limes
3 sprigs parsley, chopped
salt and pepper

Fry peppers, onions, garlic and ginger in the oil until soft. Stir in the coconut, tomato purée, rum and a little salt and pepper. Bring to the boil and stir until the mixture thickens. Stir in crab meat and reduce the heat, simmering for 5 minutes. Spoon the mixture into the crab shells, and sprinkle with lime juice. Garnish with parsley. The filled crab shells can also be quickly heated under grill to serve piping hot.

Seafood Dishes

In Graham Greene's celebrated novel, 'Our Man in Havana', the central character's daughter, Milly, is taken to Havana's famous nightclub, La Tropicana, to celebrate her 17th birthday. It was here that after a champagne celebration, the head of the Cuban Secret Service was drenched by a girl's soda siphon. One of the Club's most famous dishes is Creole Shrimp - a dish with a compelling and intense aroma.

Camarones a la Criolla - Creole Shrimp

    900 g (2lb) veined, uncooked prawns
    4 large Jalapeno chillies, seeded and finely chopped
    2 medium onions
    4 tomatoes, blanched, peeled and chopped
    2 tbs vegetable oil
    25g (1oz) peeled, finely chopped fresh ginger
    1 bay leaf
    1 tsp brown sugar
    3 drops tabasco sauce
    1 cup white wine
    small quantity chopped parsley
    pinch salt and pepper
    225g (8oz) rice

Sauté onions and chillies until soft. Add tomatoes, bay leaf, parsley, ginger, salt, pepper and sugar. Reduce heat and add prawns, cover and simmer for 10 minutes. Add tabasco, stir and serve over cooked rice.

Classic Cuban Cookery

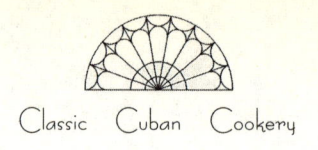

ENCHILADA DE CAMARONES – PRAWN-STUFFED TURNOVERS

    450g (1lb) peeled prawns
    1 large onion, finely chopped
    3 garlic cloves, crushed
    2 Habanero chillies, seeded and chopped fine
    1 tsp fresh coriander, chopped fine
    1/2 tsp fresh oregano, chopped fine
    1 bay leaf
    1/2 tsp cumin seeds
    2 tsp wine vinegar
    1/2 tsp ground pepper
    2 tbs tomato paste
    1 tsp salt
    1 lime
    2 tbs corn oil
    110 ml (4 fl oz) water
    6 tortillas

Squeeze the lime juice over the prawns and leave to marinate for 1/2 hour. Fry onions for 1 minute in the oil. Add garlic, chillies, coriander, and oregano. Fry for 1 minute and stir in tomato paste. Cook for 5 minutes and then add the rest of the ingredients. Cook for around 10 minutes, until prawns are cooked. Spoon prawn dish into the tortillas.

In Graham Greene's novel, 'Our Man in Havana', the main course of the diplomatic dinner served at the Hotel Nacional included Maryland Chicken and Stone Crabs. Wormold, the hero was almost poisoned with a drugged whisky at this dinner because it

Seafood Dishes

was erroneously believed that he was a spy. Graham Greene visited Cuba as a correspondent on a number of occasions between 1930 and 1950, trying to contact Fidel Castro for a story. He was a regular at the Shanghai Club and he often enjoyed the speciality of the house at the Floridita restaurant in Old Havana, which is langoustine, or spiny lobster.

LANGOUSTINE EL FLORIDITA

The sauce for this dish must be prepared in advance

>   Sauce:
>   2 medium onions, finely chopped
>   50g (2oz) butter
>   4 large Serrano chillies, finely chopped
>   1 tsp Tabasco sauce
>   3 cloves garlic, crushed
>   juice of 4 limes
>   1 tsp brown sugar
>   1/2 tsp salt

Combine onion and lime juice and set aside for an hour. Drain and reserve lime juice. Sauté onions in the butter until they are translucent. Add chillies, lime juice, garlic, sugar and salt. Cook on a low heat for 15 minutes. Stir in Tabasco sauce.

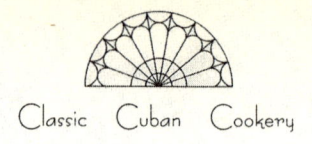

Langoustine:

900g (2lb) langoustine, cooked, carefully shelled and diced
3 small hot green chillies, finely chopped
4 tbs vegetable oil
275 ml (1/2 pint) double cream
1/2 tsp oregano
275ml (1/2 pint) white wine
small quantity of chopped parsley
225g (8oz) rice

Sauté langoustine with chillies in oil for 5 minutes. Stir well. Leaving a tablespoon of the oil in the pan, add wine and boil. Reduce heat and add sauce and oregano. Simmer for 3 minutes. Add langoustine and chillies. Cook for 10 minutes. Cook rice and place halves of shell on rice in dish. Fill shells with the mixture. Top with cream and garnish with parsley.

Turtle

Caguama is the Taino Amerindian name for the turtle. There are five varieties of turtle that live and breed in Cuba's waters. The green, loggerhead, hawksbill, carey and leatherback turtles all mate in the sea and the females come ashore between April and June to each lay around 200 eggs in the deep holes they dig on the sandy beaches. The eggs are laid at night, and take eight weeks to hatch, and the temperature of the nest determines the sex of the hatchlings. Turtle meat occasionally appears on the Cuban menu, but for the most part, the meat comes from turtles reared in captivity. The taste of turtle meat is quite similar to that of veal.

Seafood Dishes

Fricasse de Tortuga Matanzas – Matanzas Turtle Fricasse

    900g (2lb) of turtle meat, cubed (or veal if preferred)
    1 medium onion, finely chopped
    1 sweet green bell pepper, seeded and chopped
    1 garlic clove, sliced fine
    5 tbs coconut oil
    2 tbs soft brown sugar
    50g (2oz) coconut cream
    1 pint stock
    1 tsp allspice
    1 tbs extra aged rum
    3 fresh marjoram sprigs
    2 tbs flour

Fry onion, garlic and pepper in 3 tablespoons of oil. Drain vegetables, set aside. Add rest of oil to pan and sugar. Roll turtle or veal cubes in flour. Seal meat in hot sugar/oil mix, stirring. Heat the stock, and dissolve the coconut cream in it. Stir in rum. Mix all ingredients in a frying pan. Cook while covered for 15 minutes.

The original inhabitants of Cuba, the Taino Amerindians, invented many things, among which were the hammock and the canoe. Probably their most famous legacy is the barbecue. However, the meats they used are somewhat different to what the Western palate is accustomed to. Their favourite dishes were a large rodent called jutia, as well as iguana, turtle, manatee steaks and crocodile. Good sites to find your croc include the freezer sections of speciality butchers and fishmongers. Veal steak can be substituted for the crocodile, and the dish can also be made with chicken, as crocodile tastes rather like fishy chicken. Barbecued food in Cuba is known as 'Churrasco'.

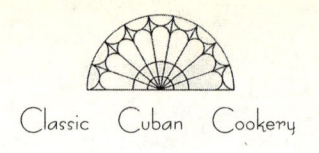

FRICASSE DE COCODRILO BARBECUE – FRICASSE OF BARBECUED CROCODILE

700g (1 1/2lb) charcoal barbecued crocodile tail steak, cubed
275 ml (1/2 pint) chicken or veal stock
1 medium sweet green bell pepper, seeded and chopped
1 medium sweet red bell pepper, seeded and chopped
25g (1oz) root ginger, peeled and chopped fine
juice of two limes
flesh of 1/2 ripe avocado, or crocodile pear, diced
2 egg yolks
175 ml (6 fl oz) double cream
1/4 tsp cayenne pepper
1/2 tsp salt
1/2 tsp brown sugar
1/4 tsp white pepper
2 tbs white rum

Mix meat and avocado and cover with lime juice and rum. Set aside. Mix stock, salt, sugar, pepper, ginger, and cayenne in saucepan. Bring stock to boil, adding peppers, reducing heat to low. Simmer for around 10 minutes, until peppers are tender. Beat egg yolks and cream together. Take the meat from the marinade. Add marinade and avocado to hot stock. Slowly stir eggs and cream mixture into stock. Add the meat, and raise the heat for 6 min-

Seafood Dishes

utes, but do not boil. Serve on a bed of rice.

If you had been in the Havana of the late 1950s, you might well be dining out with the Mob. Santo Traficante Jr. built the Hotel Capri in the late 50s, installing George Raft as manager of its Salon Roja casino, nightclub and restaurant. In 1957, Meyer Lansky built the hotel Capri, inviting Ginger Rogers to open its nightclub and restaurant, the Copa Rooms. Neither hotel has a 13th floor, as they were considered to be unlucky by the Mafia men. At Sloppy Joe's, the famous bar in Old Havana, you might have rubbed shoulders in the early 1950s with 'Lucky' Luciano, Frank Costello and Al Capone. A favourite dish of the time was Paella Cubana, which is served as a meal in its own right.

Paella Cubano

Some ingredients have to be pre-cooked. Serves 4-6.

700g (1 1/2lb) lobster meat, cooked and cubed
900g (2lb) chicken divided into 8 pieces
1 chorizo sausage, sliced
225g (8oz) tuna steak, cooked and boned
10 small clams, scrubbed and steamed
175g (6oz) shelled prawns
175g (6oz) unshelled prawns
1 medium onion, thinly sliced
1 garlic clove, finely sliced
3 tomatoes, blanched, skinned and chopped
175g (6oz) pre-cooked red beans
juice of 2 limes

Classic Cuban Cookery

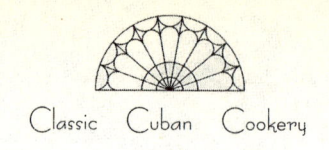

1 large sweet red bell pepper, seeded and chopped
1 large sweet green bell pepper, seeded and chopped
350g (12oz) long grain rice, pre-soaked for 30 minutes
1/4 tsp saffron, soaked in 125 ml warm water for 30 minutes
1 tsp salt
1/2 tsp black pepper
1 tsp paprika
2 tbs olive oil
570 ml (1 pint) coconut milk
pinch of nutmeg

Heat oil in large pan over moderate heat and add chicken and chorizo. Fry, turning regularly, for 15 minutes until the chicken is browned. Remove meat from pan, fry onion and garlic, until onion is soft. Add tomatoes, peppers, salt, paprika, pepper, and lime juice. Cook for 10 minutes, stirring until thick. Add rice, and cook for about 3 minutes, shaking the pan regularly. Pour in the coconut milk and saffron water mix, stirring slowly. Reduce heat and add beans, chicken pieces and chorizo. Cook for 15 minutes, stirring occasionally. Add lobster, clams, shrimps, prawns, and fish. Cook for about 5 minutes until liquid has been absorbed. Sprinkle over with nutmeg, and serve piping hot.

Classic Cuban Cookery

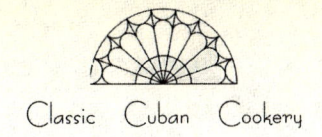

Fish Dishes

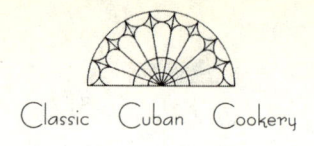

La Terraza Restaurant, Cojimar

La Terraza is just a short distance east of Cuba's capital, and was one of Hemingway's favourite haunts. It was here that he met Gregorio Fuentes, the exploits of whom inspired his book 'The Old Man and The Sea'. Gregorio captained the fishing boat 'Pilar', in which they took many trips into the 'Great Blue Stream', for more than 20 years. Fuentes was a regular at the bar, coming in nearly every lunchtime to enjoy a scotch and a fine cigar - I met him in 1986 when he was 87 years old, when he explained to me that it was his idea to call Hemingway's novel 'The Old Man and The Sea'. In recognition of his part in the writer's life, a bar in the Hemingway Marina is named 'Gregorio's' in his honour. In 1961, when 'Papa' Hemingway died, the fisherfolk ripped the brass fittings from their boats and had them melted down to make a bronze bust made in memory of the writer. The bust now stands on Cojimar promenade facing the ancient fortress. La Terraza is described in Hemingway's books and it became a restaurant on the instructions of Fidel Castro in 1972, gaining international fame for its seafood dishes. Photographs of the Nobel Prize-winning author decorate the restaurant, with its enclosed patio, which looks out over the bay side setting for his novel.

Fish Dishes

Fish in Cuba

There are around 900 different species of fish in Cuba's Atlantic Ocean and Caribbean waters, and inland reservoirs and rivers, are rich in freshwater fish. Offshore fishing often yields snook, tarpon and bonefish, while deep ocean fishes most often appear on the table. These include cherna, pargo, snapper, swordfish, tuna, marlin, barracuda, shark, flying fish and bonito. Freshwater lake and river fish include largemouth bass, black bass, trout, carp and tilapia.

There are several fish and crustacean farms on Cuba's coastline, mostly for crab, shrimp, prawns and spiny lobster, all of which are exported, although they are widely available in the cities and resort areas.

Visitors to Cuba might notice a distinct lack of fish on the traditional Cuban menu and the fact that, given the choice, most Cubans select meat in preference to fish. This is largely because in the past, it was the rich who dined on meat, leaving those less well off, normally the indigenous Cuban population to scrounge for fish. Since the revolution in 1959, meat has been made more accessible to all, and so it is no surprise that it is favoured.

Nevertheless, fish are prolific around Cuba as some of the main migratory routes pass Cuba's shores, including the famous 'Blue Stream' - the narrow stretch of water which lies between the north coast of the island, and the Florida Keys of the US. It is through these waters that famed gamefish, such as tuna, sailfish, marlin, and swordfish, make their annual migration into the Atlantic.

Classic Cuban Cookery

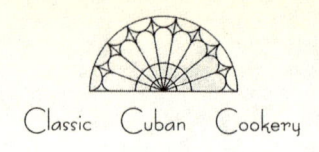

In this stretch of water, Hemingway was sailing on his yacht, 'Pilar', with the captain Gregorio Fuentes. He was fishing off his favourite island, Paraíso, when he spotted Anselmo Hernandez, an avid fisherman attempting to reel in a huge marlin. Hemingway asked Fuentes to sail the yacht nearer to the struggling fisherman, and he called out 'Can we help?' Anselmo replied with an expletive, which ended in 'Americano', and continued his fight with the fish. Hemingway noticed that Hernandez only had a bottle of water in his boat, and so, undaunted by the rebuff, he threw a bottle of rum and a couple of bocadillos, or sandwiches, into the small boat. This was the inspiration for his award winning novel, 'The Old Man and the Sea', and the old man, Santiago, was based on Hernandez, who regularly took his boat out of Cojimar harbour, near Hemingway's La Vigía mansion, to hunt the elusive marlin. He sailed away to write one of the best fishing stories ever told. Fuentes explained to me that Hemingway had asked him for a title for the manuscript, and that he, Gregorio, had said, 'you saw the old man, and the sea...'

In the 18th century, the pirates operating from the west coast of Cuba, captured a young girl in a raid on Cartagena, Columbia. They brought her back to Cuba, and built an inn for her to run, overlooking the sea. The inn became a popular port of call with the 'Brethren of the Coast', and the girl, Maria, literally grew fat on the proceeds. She acquired a nickname, 'Maria la Gorda', or 'Fat Mary', and provided the pirates with food, drink, and other 'services'. One of the dishes Maria might have offered her clientele, is Pescado en Escabeche, or Pirate's Pickled Fish.

Fish Dishes

PESCADO EN ESCABECHE – PIRATE'S PICKLED FISH

900g (2lb) filleted Cherna or Wreckfish
2 large onions, sliced thinly
1/2 sweet green bell pepper, sliced lengthways
50g (2oz) root ginger, peeled and finely chopped
1 clove garlic, finely chopped
6 tbs olive oil
225 ml (8 fl oz) malt vinegar
pinch of mace
1/4 tsp allspice
1 bay leaf
6 peppercorns
400 ml (14 fl oz) water
salt and pepper

Fry onions until golden in 110ml of oil, and remove onions from pan. Brown fish lightly in the same pan. Put fish in serving dish and cover with the onions. Add ginger, garlic, bay, peppercorns, and spices to water in pan. Season with salt and pepper. Simmer for 15 minutes. Add vinegar and remaining oil. Simmer for 2 minutes. Strain mixture over fish and onions and leave to stand overnight. Season with salt and pepper. Serve heated or cold garnished with bell pepper slices.

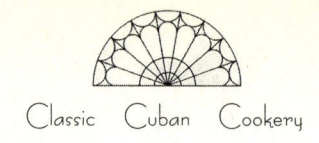

Oregano

Oregano ('Origanum onites') is a branch of the marjoram family. It is generally used in tomato and meat sauces but can also be used to flavour strong and close-textured fish. Sweet Marjoram ('Origanum magorana') is a comforting herb, used in indigestion and for tension headaches. Other medicinal uses include bringing down high blood pressure and relieving muscular aches. The Spanish name for oregano is the same as the English. Another important herb used in Afro-Cuban medicinal preparations, is known as 'Oregano Cimmarron', or runaway slave's herb.

Atun con Ron – Tuna with Rum Sauce

- 4 tuna steaks, 2cms thick
- 1 large onion, finely sliced
- 3 large tomatoes, blanched, skinned and chopped
- 2 garlic cloves, chopped fine
- 1/2 teaspoon salt
- 1/2 teaspoon ground black pepper
- 55 ml (2 fl oz) olive oil

Marinade:

- 75ml (3 fl oz) olive oil
- 75 ml (3 fl oz) gold rum
- juice of 2 limes
- 2 garlic cloves, crushed
- 1 tsp ground black pepper

Fish Dishes

1 tsp dried oregano

Mix marinade ingredients in a shallow bowl. Place tuna in bowl, basting occasionally, for 3 hours. Fry onion and garlic in oil until soft, then add tomatoes. Cook for 3 minutes. Add marinade, and simmer for 20 minutes. Rub salt and pepper into tuna steaks. Add to mixture. Cook for 10 minutes on each side. Serve with the sauce.

Basil

Basil is widely used in Cuban cookery, and was brought over to the country by the Spanish. There are over fifty types of basil, but two main varieties, Ocimum basilicum, or Sweet Basil, and Ocimum minimum or Bush Basil are used in cookery. The Spanish name for this bush herb, is 'albahaca'. Basil is traditionally used in turtle soup, and with numerous tomato dishes. Basil is also used in a snuff concoction, to clear headaches, aid digestion, and to act as a laxative. Basil vinegar can be made by infusing leaves in wine vinegar for two weeks.

Cherna Criollo – Creole-style Wreck Fish

700g (1 1/2lb) cherna or wreck fish steaks
1 large onion, chopped
2 medium tomatoes, chopped
1 red sweet bell pepper, seeded and chopped
110g (4oz) butter
5 tbs tomato sauce
1 tsp salt
1 tsp pepper

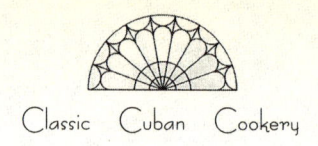

Season cleaned fish with salt and pepper. Saute fish in 50g (2oz) butter, turning until golden. Set fish aside in warm oven. Heat the remaining butter in a saucepan. Fry onions, peppers and tomatoes in pan until soft. Add tomato sauce. Simmer on low heat for 10 minutes. Pour sauce over fish. Return to pre-heated oven at 180°C (350°F) degrees for 15 minutes.

Cumin

Cumin, ('Cuminum cyminum') is originally from Egypt, and its aromatic seeds are used in many Caribbean dishes and curries. It was once of the most widely used spices in Europe in the Middle Ages, and was probably brought to Cuba with the earliest Spanish explorers. The plant only grows to 15cm height, and is at home in Cuba's climate. The seeds are easily digested and are warming to the system, and this makes them very useful medicinally as well as in the kitchen. The seeds are most commonly used to flavour meat and fish.

PARGO CUBANO – CUBAN-STYLE RED SNAPPER

1 900g (2lb) Red Snapper, cleaned and washed (leave the head on)
2 large onions, finely chopped
2 cloves garlic, crushed
2 pints tomato juice
275 ml (1/2 pint) double cream
juice of 2 limes
1 tbs brown sugar
2 tbs coconut oil
2 tsp black pepper

Fish Dishes

    2 tbs ground coriander seeds
    1 tbs Tabasco sauce

Fry onions and garlic in oil, until onions are soft. Bring tomato juice to the boil, and add to onions. Add pepper, coriander and Tabasco. Simmer for 15 minutes. Mix lime juice and sugar and stir in. Simmer for 5 minutes. Pour the cream into the middle of pan, cover and gently simmer. After 5 minutes, place the fish in the pan, on top of the sauce. Cover pan and cook slowly for 10 minutes. Turn fish over and cook for another 10 minutes. Serve with cooked rice.

Mints

The Spanish for mint is 'menta', but its Spanish botanical name is herbabuena, which is also the name for the type of mint used to make the cocktail known as Mojito. There are seven types of mint in Cuba, of which three are commonly used in the kitchen. These are spearmint, ('Mentha spicata'), peppermint ('Mentha piperita') and Pennyroyal ('Mentha pulegium'). Spearmint aids digestion, and is used in a medicinal drink, and to stimulate the appetite, and it is also the type of mint used in sauces and jellies as an accompaniment to meat. Peppermint is the source of essential oil, and is also used in peppermint tea, the mint julep and creme de menthe. The pungent pennyroyal variety was once used as a purgative for the blood.

Robalo con Salsa Verde – Bass in Green Sauce

    4 fillets of largemouth bass (or sea bass)
    large bunch fresh parsley, finely chopped
    large bunch fresh mint, chopped fine

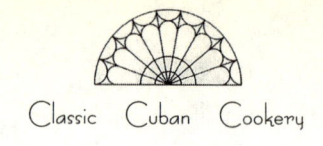

1 tsp rinsed capers, chopped
2 garlic cloves, finely sliced
1 tsp mustard
1 tbs chopped gherkins
2 shallots, finely chopped
dash of Tabasco sauce
pinch of salt and pepper
6 tbs olive oil

Fry the fish in half of the oil until golden brown both sides. Set fish aside, keep warm. Lightly fry garlic and shallots in oil. Remove from heat, and add rest of oil. Let cool, then stir in the rest of the ingredients. Whisk together to form a thick sauce. Pour sauce over fish and serve.

Pompano Platano – Banana Barbecued Pompano Fish

450g (1lb) pompano fillets, cut in 3cm strips
3 banana leaves, cleaned and washed
juice of 2 limes
1 tsp fresh ground black pepper

Marinade:
4 tbs olive oil
1/2 tsp cayenne pepper
4 dried bay leaves, crumbled into powder
2 tbs gold rum

Fish Dishes

Mix half the oil, cayenne pepper, rum, and bay powder together. Put marinade in shallow dish and place fish strips in marinade. Leave in refrigerator overnight. Remove dish and brush both sides of fish strips with marinade. Cut banana leaves into 3cm strips. Coat both sides of the banana leaf strips with rest of oil. Place a strip of fish on banana leaf strip. Roll the fish in the banana leaf strips and skewer through. Oil the rack of the heated barbecue. Cook each fish roll on barbecue for 2-3 minutes, turning. Serve on a bed of rice with a hot sauce dip.

Filete de Emporador Rebozado – Fillets of Swordfish

    4 350g (12oz) swordfish steaks
    4 sprigs fresh coriander
    8 slices lemon, halved
    juice of six limes

    Marinade:
    55 ml (2 fl oz) corn oil
    25g (1oz) salt
    1 tsp cayenne pepper
    25g (1oz) dried thyme
    25g (1oz) dried oregano
    1 tsp ground black pepper
    2 l (3 1/2) pints cold water

Mix all marinade ingredients together in large, shallow dish. Marinade swordfish steaks in the marinade mixture for 24 hours. Barbecue steaks 3 minutes on each side. Serve garnished with coriander and lemon slices.

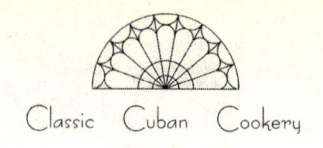

Mahi Mahi (Dolphinfish)

Known variously as Dolphin, Mahi Mahi, or Dorado, this rainbow-coloured fish is no relation to the mammalian dolphin. The Mahi Mahi, which is featured on the front cover of this book is an iridescent green-blue, with yellow, gold and purple sides. It is a fine sports fish, swimming near the surface in offshore waters, where it hunts flying fish and squid, often attaining speeds of 50 knots in chase. Mahi Mahi grows very quickly, and commonly reaches a weight of 30lbs. Not only is it one of the most colourful of sporting fish, the Dolphin's firm, white flesh, resembling that of the swordfish, is said to be one of the most delicious found in the Caribbean.

BAKED MAHI MAHI

4 450g (1lb) Mahi Mahi steaks
1 large onion, finely chopped
4 tomatoes, sliced
3 garlic cloves, crushed
2 Serrano chillies, seeded and finely chopped
2 tbs butter
juice of 2 limes
1 tbs fresh parsley, finely chopped
1/2 tbs fresh thyme, finely chopped
1 bay leaf
1 tsp salt

Fish Dishes

Mix together the garlic, chilli, lime juice, and salt. Rub mixture into both sides of each steak. Place in baking dish and place 2 tomatoes sliced on each steak. Surround with butter, parsley, thyme, onion and 2 tomato slices. Pour in around 1/2 pint of water, not quite covering fish. Bake in a hot oven for 40 minutes, basting, until the flesh of the fish is opaque.

RICE AND SPEARFISH STEAKS

    4 thin Spearfish steaks, about 75g (3oz) each
    2 sweet red bell peppers, finely chopped
    1 large onion, peeled and quartered
    110g (4oz) canned peas
    4 tbs olive oil
    2 pints fish stock
    225g (1/2 lb) rice

Sauce:
6 Jalapeno chilli peppers, finely chopped
110g (4oz) papaya flesh, finely chopped
2 large onions, finely chopped
3 cloves garlic, finely chopped
25g (1oz) root ginger, peeled and finely chopped
1/2 tsp turmeric
3 tbs malt vinegar
dash of Tabasco sauce
dash of Worcestershire sauce
1 tsp salt

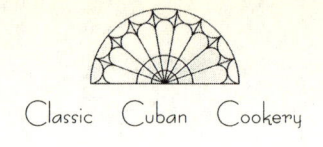

1/2 tsp pepper
1 tsp brown sugar

Sauce:
Bring to boil all ingredients in pan, stirring constantly. Reduce heat and simmer for 5 minutes. Blend or purée mixture until smooth. Fry onion quarter and bell peppers until soft. Set aside. Pour smooth sauce over fish steaks in dish. Stand for 4 hours. Clean the fish from the marinade, reserving sauce. Lightly brown fish steaks in the oil. Remove steaks from pan and saute rice in pan until light brown. Turn rice into casserole dish, and the sauce. Add peas, cooked peppers, onion, stock and fish steaks. Cover and cook for 30 minutes, or until rice and fish are done.

When Christopher Columbus arrived in Cuba, he wrote about the fishing nets and hooks used by the Taino Amerindians. The Taino would use the remora, or sucker-fish to catch larger fish. The remora attaches itself to large fish and sharks and hitch a ride, while feeding off scraps from the host fish's meal. The Taino would catch the remora and release them on a long line and wait for them to attach themselves to a larger fish, when they would draw both fish to the boat or shore. Cuba's rivers and lakes teem with fish, particularly the favoured Black, or Largemouth bass, and Trout, or Trucha. The island's early inhabitants caught these by means of a woven fish trap in the shape of a funnel. Today, the island promises visiting fishermen some of the best sea and freshwater fishing anywhere.

Fish Dishes

Trucha Taino – Taino Trout

Wash hands thoroughly after seeding chillies.

900g (2lb) trout, cleaned
3 shallots, finely chopped
1 small sweet bell pepper, finely chopped
1 jalapeno chilli, seeded and chopped fine
1 tbs olive oil
75g (3oz) coconut cream, dissolved thick in boiling water.
juice of 3 limes
1 tbs fresh coriander, chopped

In a small dish, lay fish and pour on lime juice. Leave for 1 hour. Remove fish, pat dry. Keep lime juice. In the oil, fry fish for 2 minutes each side, browning skin. Remove fish and set aside. Fry shallots, pepper, and chilli, until soft. Add coconut milk and then the fish. Simmer for around 15 minutes, or until fish is cooked.
Serve fish covered in sauce and garnished with coriander.

Classic Cuban Cookery

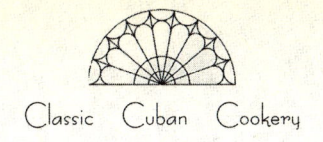

Vegetarian and Vegetable Dishes

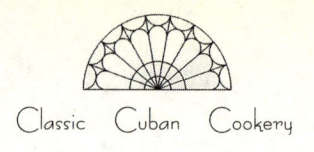

La Bodeguita Del Medio Restaurant, Havana

The Bodeguita del Medio is located at 207 Empedrado Street. In April 1942, Angel Martinez opened a grocery store here in this old carriage house adjoining the mansion of the Countess de la Reunion. Intellectuals, writers and poets would gather in the store and talk over a drop of rum, and when Angel married, his wife would cook meals in the store and friends would often join them for lunch. It gradually became a thriving eating house called Casa Martinez with 11 tables and a small bar. It became famous throughout the island and today it has extended upwards to occupy three stories and is known worldwide. Replicas of the restaurant have been built in both Italy and Spain.

Visitors have graffitied the walls - signatures of presidents, writers and actors alongside tourists and locals, and picture of the famous are also displayed. Hemingway's photograph is also up, alongside his famous quote: 'My mohito in the Bodeguita and my daiquiri in the Floridita'. The chair fixed high up on the wall in the back room is said to be reserved for a regular client who, after many years of dining here, went to sea and failed to return.

Vegetarian and Vegetable Dishes

Vegetable dishes

Both tropical and temperate vegetables are raised in the Cuban garden. The familiar cabbage, lettuce and carrot rub shoulders with yucca, eddoes, okra and peppers. The cornucopia of Cuba's vegetables also provides all the necessary vitamins, proteins and carbohydrates and, together with the country's fruit selection, can provide an ideally balanced vegetarian diet.

Spanish colonists were quick to introduce European vegetables and some fruits into their new-found islands in the 17th century and it was not long before other, more exotic plants were being imported for their seeds. Slave merchants realised that their slaves thrived better on the vegetarian diet which they were accustomed to in West Africa, and were soon bringing selected roots, tubers and seeds from Africa to their Caribbean colonies.

Cuba's sugar plantations had large plots of land set aside for vegetable and fruit cultivation and the plantation workers were allocated allotments of land on which they cultivated their native and local produce. It was the African slaves who introduced the first barter markets to Cuba, exchanging their excess produce for bread, salt pork, fish, game, cooking oils and spices. Today, co-operative farmers in Cuba are still bartering any produce left over from their government run vegetable and fruit farms.

Classic Cuban Cookery

Vegetables and Vegetarian Dishes

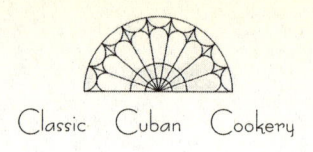

Apart from Cuba's staple diet of rice, beans and root crops, the island provides an ideal climate for raising a great variety of vegetables. Even mushrooms are grown in caves in large enough quantities to export.

Much of Cuba's diet is vegetarian by necessity. There are a number of vegetarian recipes that feature in traditional Cuban cookery, although meat is added to a dish if it is available. Few main meals are created to be entirely vegetarian, as even vegetable stews and the famous Moros y Christones (Moors and Christians) otherwise known as kidney beans and rice, will be cooked with addition of pork fat, or pieces of pork.

It is not unusual for vegetarians to ask for a dish to be cooked with purely vegetable ingredients. However, there are a number of Cuban side dishes and main meals consisting solely of vegetables, so the vegetarian visitor should always ask exactly what a dish consists of, if strict dietary requirements are to be maintained.

Cubans have a preference for dicing, cooking and canning their vegetables, resulting in what the Cubans generally call vegetable salad. If a traditional salad is required, the desired items should be listed to avoid disappointment. For instance, if a tomato salad is requested, the usual result is a plate of roughly chopped tomatoes, both green and red, and nothing else. Eggs and cheese are widely available and many restaurants serve pasta and pizza.

In the city hotels in resort areas, mayonnaise, salad oil, salad cream, ketchup and sauces familiar in bottles on western tables are usually available, but Cuban chefs also pride themselves in producing their own versions.

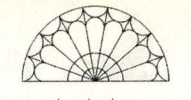

Vegetable and Vegetarian Dishes

Cassava

The Arawak tribes of Cuba had been cultivating cassava ('casbe') for centuries before the arrival of Columbus in 1492. The cassava is a bulbous, brown tuber, which was worshipped in the form of the Arawak god 'Yoca-hu', or the cassava giver. They grew the plant in small plots of land known as 'burren'. Where irrigation was poor, special mounds of earth were built, known as 'conducos'. In these, the natives planted crops requiring good drainage at the top of the mound, and those water-loving plants at the base, so that irrigation could be regulated. One species of this tuber is still called jucca, after the ancient's collective name for the plant, 'yoca'.

Cassava was the staple diet of the Arawaks, and they extracted the preservative, cassareep from it. Easy to cultivate, cassava contains a toxin, a form of prussic acid, called hydrocyanic acid, which must be eliminated from the root before it is eaten. Boiling or baking the tuber removes this toxin. Cassava flour was produced by the Amerindians, by peeling the tubers, grating them on fan coral and mixing the resulting flakes with water. The flesh was then strained through a cotton bag, which was tightened until all the cyanide-like juice was expelled. The flour produced was used to bake a large round flat bread, known as casabe. The juice from making the cassava flour was fermented to make a beer.

The ground flesh can be used to make a flour, or as a soup additive. It can also be boiled or roasted and used as a vegetable. The leaves of the cassava are also edible and are usually boiled. Cassava is the source of tapioca and arrowroot, and is high in starch, vitamin C, small amounts of vitamin B1, antioxidants, and low in protein. Cassava contains 132 calories per 100 grams. No one knows exactly which ingredients the Arawak used to make their cassava bread, but here is one possible recipe.

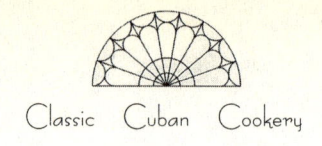

Pan de Casabe – Cassava Bread

1.8 kg (4lb) peeled and grated cassava
1 small coconut, grated meat of
450g (1lb) white sugar
110g (4oz) raisins
110g (4oz) cooking margarine
225g (8oz) butter
1 tsp allspice
1 tsp ground cinnamon
1 tsp grated nutmeg
2 tsp vanilla essence
2 tsp salt
milk for mixing

Combine all the ingredients in a large bowl and mix well. Add enough milk to make the mixture soft. Stand to one side for 15 minutes. Grease a large baking pan, and turn mixture into it. Bake in a pre-heated, 180°C (350°F) degree oven, for 1 1/2 hours.

Jucca

The jucca plant is very similar to the cassava, or yam, and is one of the most popular root vegetables in Cuba today. More often than not, jucca is cooked as a vegetable with lashings of garlic. However, the jucca can also be used in semi-sweet savoury dishes.

Vegetable and Vegetarian Dishes

Bunuelos de Jucca Cocinada Santa Ana – Santa Ana-Style Jucca Doughnuts

900g (2lb) jucca, peeled and chopped
1 egg, beaten
125 ml plain flour
1/2 tsp crushed aniseed
1/4 tsp ground cinnamon
rind of a quarter lemon
pinch of salt
1 tbs caster sugar
maize oil for frying

Cook the jucca until very soft. Place jucca in bowl and fold in egg and flour. Mix in the aniseed, cinnamon, and salt. Mix well, into a dough, and knead it on a pastry board. When firm, like bread dough, divide into 10 portions. Roll each portion into sausages around 10 inches long. Fold each sausage into 'figures of eight'. Stick ends together with a spot of water. Heat oil in deep fry pan. Deep fry each bunuelo until golden, around 1 1/2 minutes each. Drain off oil, and sprinkle with sugar. Serve bunuelos hot, decorated with curls of lemon rind.

Yam

The Taino cultivated yams ('dioscorea'), which they called 'wa wa'. There are more than 600 varieties of yam and they are all an excellent source of carbohydrate. The pure white flesh contains a calorie per gram and they can be used in many different ways as a vegetable. The Cush Cush variety, ('Dioscorea trifida'), the tastiest of all, is the only variety native to Cuba. Another yam variety, known as Name, is also raised throughout the country.

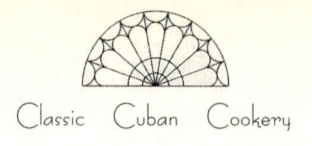

Amaranth

The Amaranth is native to the tropical Americas, and was revered by the Amerindians, who would paint themselves with the purple-red dye extracted from the flowers, to ward off evil spirits. For this reason, the Spanish destroyed any Amaranth plants they found. However, unbeknown to them, the seeds contain more protein than wheat, corn, or rice. The Aztecs too attributed magical powers to the Amaranth, offering the plants as food to their gods, together with the sacred maize cob. In some parts of the Caribbean, the leaves of this plant are known as callaloo, not to be confused with the leaves of the dasheen, which is also called callaloo. The leaves of Amaranth resemble spinach, and are rich in iron and vitamin C and are a common addition to stews.

Taro

The taro, or eddoe ('colocasia esculenta antiquorum') is a small, round, tuberous root. It was imported from Africa as a staple in the diet of the slave population. This vegetable is used in the manufacture of arrowroot and the root can be boiled or baked and the leaves can be used as a green. Eddoes contain 92 calories per 100 gram. When peeling the vegetable, wear gloves.
Eddoes are usually known as malanga in Cuba, and come in two varieties, yellow and white fleshed.
Malanga is an important ingredient in many of the country's dishes, and is often served as a side dish, cooked plain, or served with a garlic sauce.

Vegetable and Vegetarian Dishes

Malanga con Ajo – Garlic Eddoes

    450g (1lb) malanga, peeled and sliced
    4 garlic cloves, finely chopped
    3 tbs maize oil
    1tsp annatto seeds
    1 tbs white vinegar
    pinch of salt

Heat the oil with the annatto seeds to add colour and flavour. Discard annatto seeds when oil is coloured. Boil malanga in salted water for 30 minutes. Drain and dry malanga. Mix vinegar, salt, garlic and oil in a bowl. Pour mixture over hot or cold malanga and serve.

Arroz - Rice

Rice is known as arroz in Spanish and it is now one of the country's staple diets, grown widely on the Caribbean side of the island in west, central and southern Cuba. In western Cuba, where much of the country's rice is grown, the main six-lane highway is often devoid of traffic and roadside rice-growers have found that the surface of this road is ideal for drying and winnowing their crops. Rice grain has a husk and a skin, which are often removed by milling before marketing. Brown rice has only the husk removed and is more nutritious, retaining much of the proteins, minerals and vitamins. Long, short and round grain rice are the most commonly used varieties in Cuban cooking.
From the 16th century, a slow but steady stream of Chinese labour arrived in Cuba via the Manila, through Acapulco, across Mexico and from Vera Cruz to Havana and they brought rice with them. However, in the 19th century, just after Cuba abolished slavery in 1880, around 180,000 Chinese were brought to Cuba as indentured labour, from

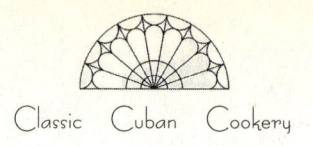

China's Guangdang province. Rice was quickly adopted by Cuba as its staple diet, although root and tuber are still widely used. There is now a thriving Chinese community in Cuba, and even a Chinatown in Havana. The introduction of rice was one of the major developments in Cuban cuisine. When cooking rice, it can treble its volume, so making it a filling and nutritious cereal.

ARROZ CON PLATANO – RICE WITH BANANAS

275g (10oz) long grain rice, soaked in water for 30 minutes
2 eggs lightly beaten
2 bananas, sliced
2 tbs maize oil
1 garlic clove, finely chopped
4 spring onions, finely chopped
juice of 1 lime
1 pint water
pinch of salt

Cook the rice in the water thoroughly and drain. Fry garlic and onions in oil until soft. Add bananas, stirring well for 2 minutes. Pour over beaten eggs. Before the eggs set, pour in the cooked rice, stirring constantly. Fry for around 3 minutes until the rice is coated with oil. Add salt and lime juice and cook for a further minute and serve hot.

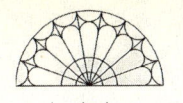

Vegetable and Vegetarian Dishes

Oil Palm

The oil palm was probably introduced to Cuba from West Africa. The oil is extracted from both the boiled and crushed flesh of the palm fruit and the kernel or palm nut. Palm wine is also extracted from the trunk by tapping the tree just below the flower stalk. The juice, or sap, which slowly seeps into a bottle ferments quickly into an alcoholic liquor. The palm oil is also used to make margarine and soap and sometimes subsidises corn or olive oil. Palm oil is sometimes substituted for corn or olive oil

ARROZ CUBANO

400g (14oz) long grain rice
2 garlic cloves, peeled and sliced fine
25 ml (1 fl oz) vegetable stock
2 tsp cumin seeds
75g (3oz) scallion onions, chopped fine
1 tbs palm oil
12g (1/2oz) ground black pepper
225g (8oz) frozen peas
225ml (8 fl oz) tomato purée
12g (1/2oz) salt
570ml (1 pint) water

Sweat scallions, garlic, salt, pepper and cumin, in oil. Add cooked mixture to raw rice, mix thoroughly. Boil water, tomato purée, and vegetable stock. Add the rice mixture and stir briefly. Simmer for 15 minutes until rice is cooked. Add peas and mix thoroughly. Serve when the peas are cooked.

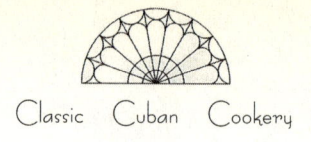

Pepitas de Cush Cush – Yam Nuggets

1 litre cooked, mashed yams
2 eggs
2 tbs milk
salt and pepper
deep fryer one third filled with cooking oil

Cook yams in salt water, then discard water and wash yams. Mash yams with a fork with eggs and milk. Form mixture into round balls, or nuggets. Deep fry nuggets in the oil until golden brown.

Beans

There is a wide variety of beans that are native to Cuba and the Americas. Beans formed a substantial part of the Arawak diet, and the generic term for beans in Spanish is 'frijoles'. Both the red and black kidney beans are most popular in Cuban cuisine - the red kidney bean, or colorado is used to make refried beans and bayos, the black kidney bean is more commonly cooked with rice. Haricot or blanco beans are also popular and are used in baked beans and stews. French beans are a common ingredient in several Cuban dishes.

Pigeon peas, or congo peas ('Cajanus cajan'), known in Cuba as 'gandules', also come from the Americas and West Africa, and grow on a shrub, about 9 foot (3 metres) in height. Pigeon peas are high in protein, fibre, iron and potassium, and form an integral part of many savoury dishes. They contain 118 calories per 100 grams. Pinto beans and flageolet beans, are not so widely used in Cuban cookery, but the American favourite, black-eyed beans, are often used in pork stews. The following recipes are for black, red, and white beans. Dried beans should be soaked in water overnight, and the brought very slowly to the boil, and then simmered for about an hour, until soft.

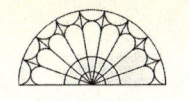

Vinales Valley is the centre of the cigar tobacco industry, where tobacco-drying sheds dot the patchwork of fields like the houses on a monopoly board. In between the tobacco crops local farmers grow their vegetables, jucca, malanga, taro, cassava and beans - red, black and white. One of the best local restaurants in the province is just outside Pinar del Rio city. It is called the Rumayor, and specialises the true Cuban dishes, like the following recipes, literally called 'bean feast'.

COMILONA FRIJOLES – CUBAN BEAN FEAST

350g (12oz) white haricot beans, soaked overnight
6 Serrano chillies, seeded and halved
1 medium onion, finely sliced
110ml (4 fl oz) olive oil
1 bay leaf
sprig of rosemary
1/4 tsp ground black pepper
pinch of salt

Combine beans, rosemary, bay, and half pepper in saucepan. Cover with water, bring to the boil, simmer for 1 hour. Add more water if required. Fry onion and chillies in oil. Add browned onions and chillies to beans. Continue to cook until beans are soft. Remove bay leaf and rosemary, and serve.

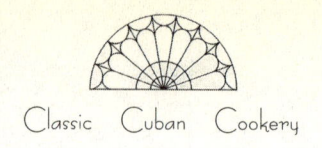

Arroz y Frijoles Colorados – Rice and Red Beans

175g (6oz) coconut cream, dissolved in
570ml (1 pint) of boiling water
225g (8oz) long grained rice
225g (8oz) dried red kidney beans, soaked and cooked
1 sweet red bell pepper, seeded and sliced lengthways
water from cooked beans
3 thyme sprigs
1 clove garlic, crushed
2 stalks spring onions, chopped fine
2 shallots, finely chopped
1/4 teaspoon pepper
1/4 teaspoon peppercorns
pinch of salt

Cover rice in pan with coconut milk. Add garlic. Bring to boil, lower heat, and cook slowly. Add water from beans as coconut milk is absorbed. Stir until liquid is almost absorbed by the rice. Add the rest of the ingredients except red pepper, to rice. Cover pan and cook. Add more water where necessary. Maintain heat until rice is completely cooked. Serve immediately, garnished with red pepper slices.

Coriander

Coriander, ('*Coriandrum sativum*'), known as 'colantro' in Spanish, has been used in culinary and medicinal circles for thousands of years. It belongs to the chervil, cumin and dill family, and has jagged feathery leaves. The leaves are used extensively in Cuban cookery, both as a decoration, in salads and as flavouring. The ripened seeds are dried crushed and are used in both savoury and dessert cookery as an aromatic and fragrant spice. Coriander also has digestive properties and was thought to be an aphrodisiac. Black beans are known as 'frijoles bayos' in Cuba.

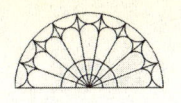

Frijoles Bayos Cilantro – Black Beans and Coriander

560g (1 1/4 lb) dry black beans, soaked in water overnight
6 tbs olive oil
25g (1oz) salt 1 tbs finely chopped, fresh coriander

Boil the beans in pan of water until soft. Simmer and reduce liquid until it is quite thick. Add olive oil, salt and coriander, and stir well. Serve hot or cold.

Moros y Christiones – Moors and Christians (Rice and Black Beans)

750ml rice
250ml black beans
3 sprigs thyme
2 tbs chopped fresh coriander
meat of one medium sized coconut, finely grated
pinch of salt
2 cloves garlic, crushed
3 spring onions
1/4 tsp ground black pepper
1 quart hot water

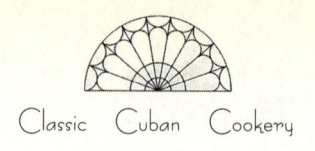

Soak beans overnight and then wash thoroughly. Add two cups of the water to the coconut. Squeeze through a sieve. Repeat this extraction of coconut milk until the water is finished. Put beans and coconut milk in a pan with the garlic. Cook until the beans are tender but not overcooked. Add spring onions, pepper, thyme, and one tablespoon of coriander. (Some cooks add a few pieces of pork at this stage). Boil for 5 minutes, then add rice and salt. Boil until the rice is done, adding more water if required. Serve sprinkled with the remainder of chopped coriander.

Batatas - Sweet Potatoes

Sweet potatoes, ('Ipomoea batatas'), or Batatas, a native of the New World, are also widely grown in Cuba. There are several different varieties of this plant, which is one of the fifteen most important food crops in the world. 'Batatas' is an Arawak word and is the basis for the word 'potato'. The name comes from the Arawak Amerindian word batatas, from where the word potato derives. The tuber's smooth skin is either white or a pale reddish colour, depending on the variety, and the flesh is usually white or orange. The flesh is mainly starch, or carbohydrate, is a good source of fibre, and also contains sugar, some protein, and vitamin A and C. Batatas are used both as a vegetable, and in desserts.

Flan Batatas Camara - Camara's Sweet Potato Flan

    900g (2lb) peeled, diced and boiled sweet potatoes
    2 eggs
    50ml milk
    2 tbs butter
    125ml grated cheese

Vegetable and Vegetarian Dishes

1/4 tsp nutmeg

Beat eggs together. Mix all ingredients together, then mix in eggs. Pour into a well greased baking dish. Preheat the oven to 180ºC (350ºF) and cook for one hour

COMILONA FRIJOLES OGUN – OGUN BEAN FEAST

350g (12oz) white haricot beans, soaked overnight
6 Serrano chillies, seeded and halved
1 medium onion, sliced fine
4 fluid ounces of olive oil
1 bay leaf
sprig of rosemary
1/4 tsp ground black pepper
pinch of salt

Combine beans, rosemary, bay, and half pepper in saucepan. Cover with water, bring to the boil, simmer for 1 hour. Add more water if required. Fry onion and chillies in oil. Add browned onions and chillies to beans. Continue to cook until beans are soft. Remove bay leaf and rosemary, and serve.

Garlic

Garlic ('Allium sativum'), or 'ajo' in Spanish, a native of Asia, was brought to the New World by the first Spanish settlers. A member of the lily, onion, chives, shallot, and leek family, the garlic bulb, which grows underground, consists of a cluster of cloves, held together with a papery skin. The skin of the bulb and clove is removed, and the clove is *either chopped finely, crushed in a press, or pounded in a mortar. When crushed, the garlic clove releases a pungent oil, an important ingredient in many sauces and dressings, and for making garlic butter. Garlic is rich in vitamins B1 and C and has antiseptic properties. It has many medicinal uses, including in the treatment of digestive disorders, respiratory complaints, and high blood pressure. It is also said to be an anticoagulant, an antibacterial, and an aphrodisiac. It is said to lower blood cholesterol levels and the sulphides contained in garlic are thought to prevent some cancers. Those who do not add garlic to their meals, will soon experience the anti-social qualities of the garlic on the Cuban breath, but parsley is an effective antidote to the smell of garlic. Garlic oil, which basically includes olive oil, lemon juice and salt, plus pounded garlic, is widely used in Spanish and Cuban cookery, and is known as alioli. This is sometimes made with egg yolk, and can be stored in an airtight jar.*

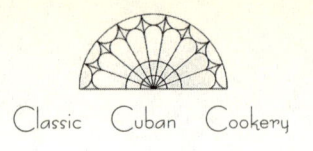

ALIOLI – GARLIC MAYONNAISE

    4 cloves garlic
    1 egg yolk
    175ml (6 fl oz) extra virgin oil
    1 tbs lime juice
    1 tsp salt

Crush the garlic with the salt. Thoroughly stir in the egg yolk. Add the oil drop by drop, stirring all the time. After one ounce has been mixed in, add the oil in a steady stream. Stir constantly and add the lime juice, stirring in thoroughly.

Vegetable and Vegetarian Dishes

Garlic Puree

    4 large heads garlic
    110ml (4oz) extra virgin olive oil
    2 bay leaves
    pinch of dried thyme

Slice garlic cloves in half. Place in a baking dish, with the sliced sides facing upwards. Sprinkle olive oil over garlic. Place bay and thyme in the dish. Bake in a hot oven for 40 minutes. Remove dish from oven. Scoop flesh from the garlic skins and mash the garlic into a purée.

Thyme

An aromatic herb, thyme ('Thymus vulgaris'), has a number of uses, and can flavour anything from chicken and veal, to vegetables, game, and fish. It is a particularly pungent herb, and can be used in a bouquet garnis with other herbs. This ancient, European herb, imported with the Spanish colonists, is also a therapeutic herb, with antiseptic and antibiotic qualities. Bacterial, fungal, and viral infections can be treated both internally and externally with preparations made with this herb. It is a digestive remedy for stomach cramps and diarrhoea, and is used to treat colds and influenza. Tomillo is the Spanish name for this herb.

Tamales Vegetariano – Vegetarian Tamales

    6 fresh cobs of maize (corn), cleaned and prepared
    whole husks of 15 maize (corn) cobs

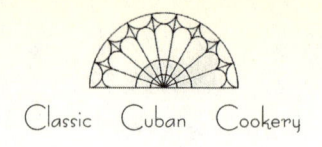

1 large onion, finely chopped
6 cloves garlic, finely chopped
2 Jalapeno chillies, seeded and chopped fine
1 green sweet bell pepper, seeded and chopped fine
65 ml (1/4 cup) butter
65 ml (1/4 cup) maize oil
2 spring onions, finely chopped
1 tsp mixed herbs
2 gherkins, chopped fine
4 olives, chopped fine
1 tsp capers
2 tbs tomato purée
pinch of salt and black ground pepper

Cut thin strips out of 4 husks, for tying tamales. Fry onion, garlic, chillies and pepper for about 10 minutes. Add herbs, capers, gherkins, olives, and tomato purée. Season with salt and pepper, and cook for 4 minutes. Grate the maize cob kernels finely, into a basin. Stir the fried mixture into the grated maize. Mix well. Place 3 corn husks flat, overlapping the two centre edges. Arrange them to form a pointed tube. Fold the pointed end of the tube up, to close it at one end. Spoon mixture into top of tube, holding the tube together. Take three more husks to close the top. Place these, pointed ends up, around the filled tube. The husks' pointed ends should stand proud of the filled tube. Hold the filled tube enclosed by the husks, upright. Fold the projecting pointed end in, to seal the top. Take a long strip of husk, and tie around tamale 'waist'. Take another long strip, and tie vertically. Boil a pan of water, and dip tamales in water. Boil for 30 minutes, until contents are firm. When cooked, drain and serve hot.

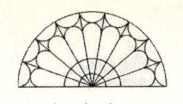

Vegetable and Vegetarian Dishes

Rosemary

This popular culinary herb, ('Rosmarinus officinalis'), has numerous culinary uses, and is particularly good with lamb and roast pork dishes. Rosemary came from Spain with the early colonists, and is said to improve the memory. An oil derived from rosemary, is made into a tonic for digestive, nervous, and circulatory problems. The oil is also used to treat hair loss, wind, headaches, and arthritis. The Spanish for this herb is 'romero'.

TOSTONES DE PLATANO VERDE – TOASTED PLANTAIN

4 plantains, sliced into finger thick slices
1 pint corn oil in deep fryer
2 tsp salt dissolved in 1 pint of water
55ml olive oil
2 cloves of garlic, finely chopped

Soak plantain slices in salt water for 10 minutes. Pre-heat oil to 180°C (350°F). Drain plantain slices and deep fry for 10 minutes. Remove slices from oil, place on chopping board. Flatten out each plantain slice. Fry slices again until golden brown and crisp. Mix olive oil and chopped garlic together. Pour the mixture over the hot plantain slices.

Aubergine

The Aubergine, 'Berenjena' in Spanish, or eggplant grows well in Cuba, and is one of the earliest vegetable imports from Europe. It is a member of the potato family, and indigenous to Asia, but was imported to Cuba with the Spanish. The fruit can be dark purple, mauve, yellow, or white. Although this is a fruit, it is cooked as a vegetable, and combined with onion, garlic, and pepper, is considered an aphrodisiac. The aubergine's flesh is often salted for a while, and then drained, to remove the bitterness and moisture.

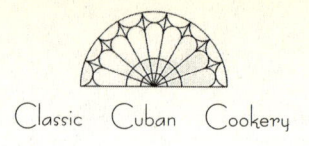

Bolas de Berenjena – Aubergine Balls

1 medium aubergine
225g (8oz) flour
1 tsp baking powder
1 tsp granulated sugar
1 tsp butter
1/2 tsp ground cinnamon
150 ml (1/4 pint) milk
salt and pepper

Peel and grate aubergine. Rub the butter into the flour. Add baking powder, sugar, cinnamon. Add grated aubergine. Mix into a soft dough by adding the milk slowly. Scoop out teaspoon-size dough balls and drop in soup or hot water.

Tortilla Espanola – Spanish-style Omelette

2 large potatoes, peeled and cut into small cubes
2 large onions, peeled and coarsely chopped
2 garlic cloves, crushed
6 eggs
1 tsp mixed dried herbs
1 tbs salad cream
dash of Tabasco sauce

Vegetable and Vegetarian Dishes

3 tbs olive oil
pinch of salt and pepper

Cook potatoes, garlic, and onion in oil for around twenty minutes. Whisk together eggs, salad cream, Tabasco, salt, pepper and herbs. Drain most of oil from pan, and add potatoes and onion to mixture. Add a little oil to a large frying pan and heat. Pour mixture into hot oil, tilt pan so that mixture fills pan. Cook for 5 minutes, shaking pan to prevent sticking. Slide tortilla onto plate, and return to pan inverted. Cook for another 5 minutes until tortilla is firm and browned.

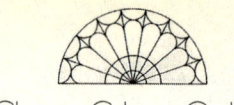

Classic Cuban Cookery

Classic Cuban Cookery

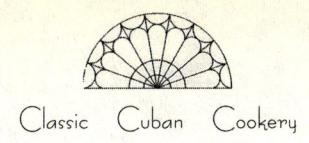

Desserts

Classic Cuban Cookery

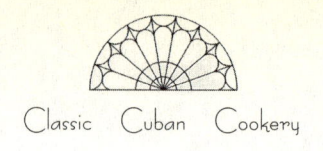

The San Carlos Cabana Fort, Havana

La Fortelaza San Carlos de la Cabana is a massive structure, which is around a tenth the size of the entire area of Old Havana. The Fortress of the Cabana, sometimes known as San Pedro, or San Carlos de la Cabana, was built between November 1763 and 1774 by Pedro de Medina, on the designs of architect Juan Bautista Antonelli and Silvestre Abarca. The fort was named after King Carlos III of Spain, and was considered to be the most important fortification in the New World. It could house 5,000 soldiers and had gun emplacements facing both East and West.

The Cabana was originally a dreaded prison and place of execution for political prisoners until the 1950s when it became a military academy. A graveyard is located to the south of the fort. Some of the young revolutionaries who were captured after the failed storming of the Mocanda Barracks in Santiago de Cuba, in July 26 1953, were incarcerated and tortured here. In the early days of 1959, Che Guevara's troops captured the fort and flew the revolutionary flag from its battlements in defiance just before Fidel Castro's triumphantly marched into the city. The fort is now an historical study centre and museum of military history. Visit La Divina Pastora, which serves seafood dishes.

Cuba's Sweet Tooth - Desserts in Cuba

'It is perhaps in the sherbets that the Havana confectioners will be found by visitors to excel. All the native fruits that can possibly be adapted to the purpose are put in requisition and in their infinite variety the most fastidious palate will not fail to find something to please.'
Handbook for Havana, CD Tyng, 1868

This extract from a century and a half ago ideally illustrates the Cuban devotion to sugar, and anything sweet and sugary. Cuba is the largest producer of sugar in the world, and

Desserts

before the harvest the land is covered in blanket of waving, green sugar cane.

Sugar cane is eaten, or rather chewed, raw from the field. The outer hard bark of the stalk is stripped away, usually with the teeth and the pithy sweet centre is crushed between the teeth and the juice released. Some traditional restaurants have a guarapo press, which is rather like an old mangle with metal teeth in the rollers. This hand operated press is used for extracting the greenish sugar cane juice, known as guarapo. This refreshing sweet juice is drunk neat, or with the addition of a tot of rum.

One of Cuba's most celebrated desserts is their Helado, or ice cream. Made entirely with natural produce and with fresh fruits of around 90 different varieties, Cuban ice creams in Cuba, is the Copelia chain, the largest outlet of which is in the park in central Havana. At times, thousands of ice cream addicts queue for a paper cone of guanavana, zapote, guava, mango, pineapple, pistachio, or coffee ice cream.

Classic Cuban Cookery

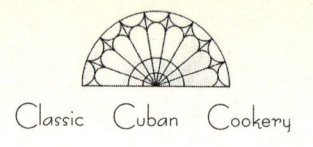

Desserts in Cuba

Almost all traditional Cuban desserts are rich in sugar. Crème caramels, known as 'natilla' are popular, flavoured with vanilla. A very sweet paste is made with guavas and this is usually eaten in a bun with cheese. This is known as pastelito de guayaba con queso. 'Dulce' is the word for candied fruit, also a popular sweet, and an egg custard, is known as a flan.

Both chocolate and coconut are used in Cuban desserts and fruit or chocolate custards, sorbets and souffles are common sweets. Tatainoff is a tasty chocolate cake and coco rallado y queso is grated coconut with cheese in a very sweet syrup. Cucurucho is a mixture of grated coconut, fruits, chocolate covered in grated coconut, and coco quemado is a sweet coconut pudding.

The best known Cuban dessert is, however, the country's famed 'helado', or ice cream. In most towns there are ice-cream dispensers known as Coppelias. Cuban ice creams, which have won international gold medals, are made with all manner of delicious fresh ingredients, from pistachio to passionfruit, and from pineapple to pomegranate.

Desserts

Banana

The Latin name for the banana, 'Musa sapientum', means 'muse of the wise man'. In 1516, Friar Thomas de Berlanga wisely introduced the banana and plantain to the nearby island of Hispaniola from the Canary Islands. Both fruits quickly found their way to Cuba and were used by the slave population as an excellent complement to their diet of cassava and other tubers. In the 19th century, a great number of Canarios emigrated to Cuba from the Canary islands, and they began serious cultivation of the plants which had been introduced 300 years earlier.

There are more than 300 different varieties of banana, which are known as Plátano in Cuba. Some of these bananas are sweet in flavour, while others are savoury or bland. The banana plant can grow up to 6 metres in height, but it can only sprout one new plant before it dies. This stem can produce up to 150 bananas, weighing up to 80lbs. Bananas contain high levels of potassium and carbohydrates, are rich in vitamin C, and low in protein and fat. Bananas also contain 94 calories per 100 gram of fruit. The dark purple petals of the male flower, can be peeled away to reveal the edible 'heart', which can be included in salads. They can also be cooked in boiling water for 20 minutes, when the outer purple petals are discarded, and the centre eaten like artichoke leaves. The large, shiny banana leaf, can be used to wrap meat or fish, for cooking, or steaming, in banana leaf 'parcels', which adds a delicate favour to the food.

PAN DE PLATANO – BANANA BREAD

- 450 g (1lb) very ripe bananas
- 4 eggs
- 450g (1lb) flour
- 450g (1lb) brown sugar
- 110g (4oz) corn oil

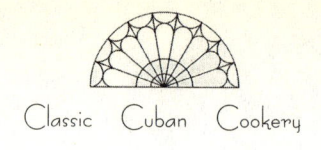

5 fl oz (1/4 pint) cream
1/4 tsp salt
1/2 oz baking soda

Blend the skinned bananas, sugar, salt and baking powder. Slowly add eggs and flour, then oil and cream. Mix well and pour into baking dish, lined with greaseproof paper. Preheat oven to 300 degrees. Bake for one and a quarter hours.

In 'The Autobiography of a Runaway Slave' by the Cuban writer, Esteban Montejo, the author describes how a man would court a girl in old time Havana. The girl would stand outside her house, watching the world go by. When her suitor passed, he would whistle to her, and as he passed, he would throw a few grains of maize towards her. If the girl fancied the man, she would pick up the maize. Later, when the two happened to meet, the girl would hold out her hand to show her suitor that she had kept the corn. The maize symbolised fertility and the man's ability to support a family. Maize, or Indian corn features in several Cuban recipes, like this country-style banana bread.

BATABANO BANANA BREAD

225g (8oz) maize flour
110g (4oz) butter
2 large ripe bananas
110g (4oz) soft brown sugar
1 egg
1 tbs baking powder
1/2 tsp salt
1 tsp allspice

Desserts

1 tsp vanilla essence
75g (3oz) raisins
2 fl oz gold rum

Preheat the oven to 180°C (350°F). Grease bread tin 20cm x 12cm. Mix butter and sugar together in a bowl. Beat in the egg and stir in the rum. Separately mash vanilla essence of bananas. Separately sift flour, nutmeg and salt into a bowl. Bit by bit, beat flour and banana mixture into butter and sugar. Roll raisins in a little flour and add to mixture. Pour batter into bread tin. Bake for 1 hour and test with a skewer, which should come out clean. Serve hot or cold.

Cocoa

The cocoa tree ('Theobroma cacao') is grown as a commercial crop throughout the tropics. It is indigenous to Central and South America and it required a warm and humid climate with plenty of rainfall - at least 150cm per annum. The majority of cocoa is raised commercially in West Africa and Central and South America, and the mountains of southern Cuba provide ideal conditions. The pink star-shaped cocoa flowers yield fruit, which grow in clusters from the tree's trunk and its larger branches. The large, oval, pulpy pods of the Cacao tree produce around 20-50 almond-shaped beans from which chocolate and cocoa is made. The pods can grow to around 40 cm in length and can vary from yellow to red when ripe. The pods can take about six months to mature.
When ripe, the pods are cut from the tree and are split open to reveal the tightly packed white seeds or beans, which are surrounded by a sweet white pulp. The beans are scooped out, separated from each other by hand and heaped in piles to ferment under banana leaves, which protect the beans from the rain and help retain the heat to enable the fermentation. During this time, the flavour of the cocoa is developed and the beans turn dull red, and the by-product of fermentation - alcohol - is drained off, often to be collected

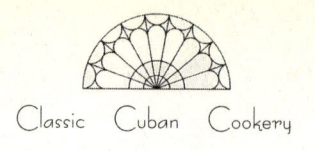

by the plantation workers. After five or six days, the beans are transformed into a wet mass, and they are dried in large revolving drums. During roasting, the shell of the beans become brittle and they are kibbled (crushed) to release the kernels. They are then ground using steel rollers. During the process, cocoa butter, which is a shiny creamy liquid is produced, and the dark paste that also results is known as chocolate liquor. The paste cools and solidifies and becomes known as cocoa mass; this is cooking chocolate and it forms the basis for all chocolate and cocoa. This mass is then squeezed to extract more cocoa butter. When about half the cocoa butter is removed, the remaining block is cocoa, which can then be ground to produce the familiar dark powder. One cocoa tree yields only one pound of pure cocoa. To make chocolate, extra cocoa butter and sugar is added to the ground cocoa solids. If only cocoa butter is added, white chocolate is made. To make milk chocolate, milk is added to the cocoa and the mixture is then dried to produce crumb. More cocoa butter is then added to the crumb and this is ground once more before being pressed into shape.

Chocolate is rich in vitamins B and D, calcium, magnesium and contains caffeine. It also contains 4% protein and 31% fat, and is one of the richest sources of iron. Chocolate has 500 calories per 100 grams in weight and is rich in an antioxidant called phenol, which is said to reduce congestion in arteries. Chocolate is used medicinally in the treatment of kidney disorders and high blood pressure. Because chocolate also contains small amounts of phenylethylamine, a chemical produced in the brain during amorous activity, it is suggested that chocolate can be an effective aphrodisiac. In the 18th century, one expert claimed that his wife had given birth to three sets of twins after indulging in copious amounts of chocolate!

Chocolate Banana Barbara

6 firm bananas peeled and sliced lengthways
50g (2oz) butter

Desserts

50g(2oz) brown sugar
juice of one lime
1/4 tsp ground cinnamon
1/2 tsp ground nutmeg
1/2 tsp vanilla essence
grated rind of 1 orange
1 tbs sweet dark coffee
55ml (2 fl oz) Anejo rum

Sauce:
350g (12oz) dark cooking chocolate
570ml (1 pint) double cream
4 egg whites
2 tbs dark, sweet coffee
25ml (1 fl oz) Anejo rum
3 tbs grated chocolate

Melt butter slowly in pan. Add bananas, sprinkling with sugar, cinnamon, lime juice and nutmeg. Fry bananas in mixture for 3 minutes, turning regularly. Add vanilla essence, coffee, and orange rind. Reduce heat and add rum. Light rum carefully to burn alcohol off. Remove from heat. Pour off and save liquid.

For the covering, melt chocolate in a separate pan. Mix in the rum. Remove from heat, stir in the coffee and half the cream. Leave to cool. Whisk egg whites until they are stiff and fold the chocolate mixture into the egg whites. Beat the remaining cream and fold into the mixture. Chill in refrigerator. Place the bananas in a heated serving dish. Pour banana liquid over them, spoon the covering over bananas and decorate with grated chocolate.

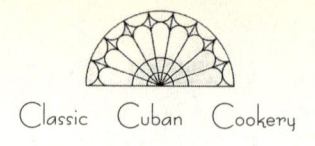

Banana Cubana – Cuban Bananas

6 ripe bananas, peeled and halved lengthways
50g (2oz) butter
8 dried cardamom pods, crushed
juice of two limes
juice of three oranges
2 tbs brown sugar
1 tbs honey
2 tbs Anejo rum
enough ice cream for four servings

Fry the banana halves in butter until gold both sides. Remove from pan and set aside. Remove pan from heat and add cardamom, juices and sugar. Bring to boil and dissolve sugar in mixture. Stir in honey when bubbling, then pour in rum. Bring to boil again and remove from heat. Pour mixture over bananas. Serve with ice cream.

Coconut

The coconut ('cocos nucifera') has taken root in just about every tropical shore. Whether the coconut arrived in Cuba on the sea currents from West Africa, or from Asia, is not known. But the tree is indigenous to Pacific Polynesia. Coconut palms have been cultivated for over 200 years and is one of the most versatile plants - not only does it provide food, its fronds can be used for thatching, baskets and brooms. The fibrous husk, coir, is used to make matting and the hard shell of the kernel is used to make utensils and charcoal. The refreshing milk and jelly inside is delicious, and even this can be dried to make copra, which is a raw material for oil and soap. While the kernel is maturing, the

Desserts

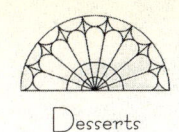

jelly becomes a harder flesh and the water becomes a sweet milk, which contains just 18 calories per 100 grams. The meat however, is the most calorific food from the vegetable world with 296 calories per 100 grams. The stalks of the coconut flowers can be tapped to yield a fermentable liquid and the flowers provide food for honey bees. Nutritionally, the coconut is a fine source of iron and phosphorous and it has many culinary uses, including forming the basis for many drinks and confectionery. One classic Cuban sweet is made from grated coconut and local honey in Baracoa, southern Cuba. This delicacy is wrapped in a triangular package made of banana leaf, and known as 'cucurucho'.

PASTEL DE CREMA COCO – COCONUT CREAM PIE

500ml freshly grated coconut
250ml granulated sugar
125ml cornstarch
3 beaten egg yolks
250ml thick cream
1/4 tsp salt
750ml hot milk
1 tsp vanilla essence
1/2 tsp almond essence
1/4 tsp allspice
1 23cm (9-inch) pie shell, previously baked

Combine sugar, cornstarch and salt in a bowl. Gradually add mixture to hot milk in a saucepan. Stir until mixture is smooth. Bring to boil whilst stirring, and boil for 2 minutes. Remove from heat and stir some into the egg yolks. Combine with the rest of the mixture in saucepan. Cook over rising heat, stirring until mixture boils. Boil for about five minutes until mixture thickens. Turn into bowl, stirring in essences and allspice. Stir in half the grated coconut. Cover mixture in greaseproof paper and freeze for 1 hour. Turn out mixture into pie crust. Spread the whipped cream evenly over the mixture. Decorate top with the rest of the grated coconut.

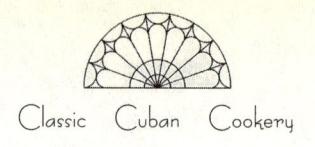

Helado de Coco – Coconut Ice Cream

>   225ml (8 fl oz) fresh coconut milk
>   225ml (8 fl oz) milk
>   225ml (8 fl oz) sugar
>   3 tbs cornflour
>   2 tbs grated coconut
>   2 egg whites, beaten until stiff
>   1/4 tsp salt

Mix the cornflour into half the milk. Mix the coconut milk with the other half of the milk. Combine the two in a pan, and add salt and sugar. Cook gently, stirring constantly, until thick. Remove from heat and stir in grated coconut. Let cool, then pour into a dish, and place in freezer. When almost frozen, take out of freezer and beat in egg whites. When the mixture is smooth, return to freezer. Remove after 3 hours, and beat again until smooth. Return to freezer and freeze solid.

Date Palm

The first of the many different varieties of date palm was probably introduced to Cuba for its decorative qualities. The Canary Island date palm is the most impressive variety and is hardy enough to survive in the sometimes cool climate of Cuba.

Desserts

Pudin Diplomatico – Cuban Bread and Butter Pudding

1 small plain sponge cake, sliced
8 egg yolks
175g (6oz) caster sugar
50g (2oz) seedless raisins (or dates)
50g (2oz) butter
275ml (1/2 pint) double cream
275ml (1/2 pint) milk
1 vanilla pod, split
1/4 tsp allspice
2 tsp gold rum
1/2 pineapple, prepared and diced

Grease a 1.75 litre (3 pint) pudding dish with part of butter. Butter the cake slices with the rest of the butter. Thoroughly mix egg yolks and 150g (5oz) of sugar together. Bring mixture of milk, cream, allspice, and vanilla pod to simmer. Strain mixture onto eggs and sugar. Mix thoroughly. Place pineapple chunks in bottom of puddling dish. Cover with rum. Arrange cake slices in layers on pineapple. Sprinkle raisins between layers. Use no raisins on final layer. Pour custard mixture over cake. Leave for 15 minutes. Place dish in tray half filled with warm water. Put both in pre-heated 180°C (350°F) oven and cook for 20 minutes. Remove from oven and sprinkle on rest of sugar. Glaze under grill.

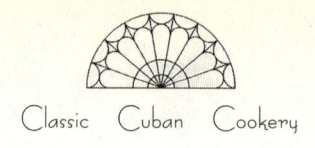

Guanabana (Soursop)

This large, green-skinned fruit, ('Annona muricata'), is part of the southern American family of anona, or cherimoya, of which there are around sixty varieties. Also known as the Soursop, this particularly delicious fruit grows on a small tree, which grows to around 20 foot in height, and the fruit can weigh up to 8lbs. The soft, prickly-skinned, Guanabana, has a firm, creamy white flesh, and is generally pear-shaped. The fibrous flesh, which is dotted with small, bright black seeds, can be eaten raw, and is used to flavour drinks and ice cream. To produce a delightfully refreshing drink from the Guanabana, mix the pulped and sieved juice with milk and add ground nutmeg, or allspice.

Guanabana Souffle

225g (8oz) Guanabana flesh, skinned and seeded
235 ml (12 fl oz) whipped cream
4 egg yolks
3 egg whites, whisked
juice of half a lime
175g (6oz) caster sugar
10g (1/2oz) gelatine
pinch of allspice

Boil a pan of water and turn the heat down. Whisk egg yolks thoroughly in a bowl over hot water. Dissolve the gelatine in 110ml (4 fl oz) of the hot water. Stir the gelatine mixture into the egg yolk mix and let cool. Whisk the cream until firm. Add enough of the lime juice to fruit pulp to flavour it. Fold the cream and the then the fruit pulp into the egg yolk mix. Fold egg whites into the mixture. Sprinkle a little allspice into moulds and fill with mixture. Place the souffles in the fridge and turn out before serving.

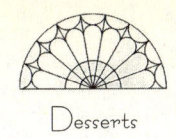

Cherimoya

The cherimoya, ('Annona cherimola'), Anon, or Sweetsop is considered one of the most delicious of Cuba's native fruits. It is green on the outside and seductively sweet and white on the inside. It has a flavour similar to the pineapple, and can be eaten raw. The fruit, which resembles a fleshy pine cone, can grow to about 10 centimetres in length. It ripens from October to May when its scaly-looking skin turns a dark green to black. As with all the Anona family of fruits, the cherimoya is a good source of thiamin, niacin, and phosphorous. Its delicate, creamy, white flesh, is used with cream and milk in dessert recipes.

Custard Apple

The custard apple, ('Annona squamosa'), or sugar apple, is also of the same family as the soursop, and the tree grows to a height of thirty-five feet, with oblong leaves, three to five inches long, and one to two inches wide. The flowers are greenish. The yellow flesh of this fruit has roughly the same taste and usage as the guanabana, or the cherimoya, although it is much sweeter, and can be eaten raw, or used as a flavouring. Because of its shape, the fruit is known as the Bullock's Heart, or 'Corozón', in Spanish.

CHAMPOLA DE CHERIMOYA - CHERIMOYA ICE

    2 ripe cherimoyas or custard apples
    450g (1lb) granulated sugar
    1/4 tsp ground cloves

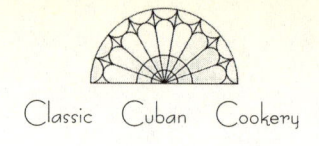

1/4 tsp allspice
225 ml (8 fl oz) water

Peel and seed the cherimoya. Purée the flesh in a blender. Boil sugar and water together for 5 minutes. Add the spices to the sugar water. Stir the syrup into the puréed cherimoya. Pour into freezer trays and stir every half hour until frozen. Serve with a liqueur topping of choice.

SOUFFLE DE CORAZON – SUGAR APPLE SOUFFLE

225g (8oz) corazon flesh (or custard apple), skinned and seeded
225 ml (12 fl oz) whipped cream
4 egg yolks
3 egg whites, whisked
juice of half a lime
175g (6oz) caster sugar
10g (1/2oz) gelatine
pinch of allspice

Boil a pan of water and turn the heat down. Whisk the egg yolks and sugar thoroughly in a bowl over hot water. Dissolve gelatine in 4 fl oz hot water. Stir gelatine mixture into egg yolk mix and let cool. Whisk the cream until firm. Add enough of the lime juice to the fruit pulp to flavour it. Fold the cream and then the fruit pulp into the egg yolk mix. Fold egg whites into the mixture. Sprinkle a little allspice into the moulds and fill with the mixture. Chill moulds and turn out to serve.

Desserts

Carambola

The carambola, or star fruit, ('Averrhoea carambola'), is a translucent, yellow fruit, which resembles a five-pointed star in cross-section. The fruit is most often used in a fruit salad, or eaten raw. It has a high vitamin C content, and contains 20 calories per 100 grams. Its cousin, the Bilimbi ('Averrhoea bilimbi'), which is a green version of the fruit, is always eaten cooked, or pickled.

ENSALADA ESTRELLA – STAR-SPANGLED SALAD

1 ripe Carambola
16 large lettuce leaves, washed and dried
4 rings of fresh pineapple cored
segments of 2 oranges, pips removed
1 grapefruit, peeled
2 peaches, stoned, skinned and quartered
2 medium tomatoes, scalded and peeled
1 tbs chopped chives
2 tsp chopped mint
juice of one lime
pinch of salt
225g (8oz) double cream
2 tbs fine grated cheese
1 tsp pimenton, or Spanish paprika

Arrange 4 lettuce leaves on each of four plates. Mix chives and cream together, add salt to taste. Place a pineapple ring on centre of each bed of lettuce. Place 2 peach quarters each side of the pineapple rings. Divide the orange segments between the four plates. Slice grapefruit vertically, de-pip, and half slices. Arrange grapefruit slices around pineapple. Quarter the tomatoes and arrange these on salads. Mix lime juice and mint together, and spoon over salads. Spoon double cream onto pineapple rings. Sprinkle grated cheese lightly over salads. Slice carambola into 12 star-shaped rings. Arrange 3 carambola stars on each salad. Sprinkle lightly with pimenton.

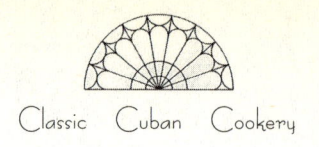

Guava

The Guava, ('Psidium guajava'), is native to Cuba, and often served as a jam, paste, or made into guava cheese. Rich in vitamin C, the tough skinned guava, which is really a large berry, turns from green to yellow when ripening, and matures throughout the year. The delicate flesh contains many tiny, edible seeds, and it is commonly eaten raw. The scented aroma of the ripe fruit can pervade a room, but the guava's taste bears no comparison to its smell. Guava is sometimes known as Guayabillo. Another species of the guava is the oval-shaped, green Feijoa, also a native New World fruit. In Cuba, a local dessert is guava jam with cheese. In Pinar del Rio province, a small, slightly bitter guava, the Guayabita, is cultivated especially for the preparation of a special liqueur, called 'Guayabita del Pinar'.

GUAVA CRISP

900g (2lbs) guava, stewed and slightly sweetened
6 tbs butter
1/2 tsp cinnamon
125ml granulated sugar
125ml flour

Desserts

275ml (1/2 pint) thick coconut milk

Put stewed guavas in a casserole dish and sprinkle with cinnamon, Combine the flour, sugar and butter in a bowl and rub into a crumble mixture. Spread the mixture evenly over the guavas and bake in a moderate oven (180°C or 350°F) for one hour. Serve hot, topped with coconut milk.

PASTELES GUAYABA

6 guavas, peeled, seeded and sliced
1 tbs butter
350g (12oz) plain flour
225g (8oz) margarine, diced small
1/4 tsp baking soda
1/2 tsp cinnamon powder
150g (5oz) granulated sugar
1 1/2 tsp salt
175 ml (6 fl oz) milk
225 ml (8 fl oz) water

Combine the flour, baking soda and salt in a bowl. Rub in the margarine until a crumble is formed. Add 110ml (4 fl oz) milk and knead into a dough. Place dough in the fridge for 1 hour. Mix guavas, sugar, water and butter in pan. Boil until the liquid has boiled off. Take off the heat and let cool. Roll out the pastry and cut into 9 flat squares. Place 2 tbs of guava mixture on one side of each square. Fold the remaining side over. Moisten the edges and seal. Brush pasteles with the remaining milk. Bake in an oven pre-heated to 180°C (350°F) until golden brown.

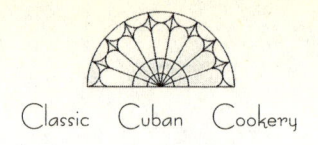

Guava Gelatima Guama – Guava Jelly

1.8 kg (4lbs) guava
150 ml (6 fl oz) water
900g (2lbs) granulated sugar
2 tsp lime juice
1/4 tsp allspice

Place the guava, allspice and water in a pan and bring to the boil. Lower the heat and simmer for 30 minutes. Whilst simmering, mash the fruit into a pulp. Make a bag of cheesecloth, tying it over a large bowl. Tying the corners to the legs of an upturned stool is ideal. Fill the bag with the pulp and leave to drain overnight. After 12 hours, discard the pulp and measure the juice. Add a teaspoon of lime and a pound of sugar to every pint. Dissolve the sugar with the lime in the juice over a low heat. Bring to the boil and keep boiling for 10 minutes. Skim foam from jelly and bottle.

Limes

Citrus fruits are a relatively recent introduction to Cuba. Sailors of the old Spanish Main were susceptible the debilitating disease, scurvy. In 1753, a ship's doctor realised that it was a lack of vitamin C that precipitated the symptoms, and lime was quickly discovered to be the best source of the vitamin. As a result, limes became widely cultivated in the Caribbean to cater for the long return journey to Europe. Cuba's crop is by far the largest in the Caribbean, and it is widely used in recipes, which are exported. Limes are known as limon in Cuba and are used for flavouring many dishes.

Desserts

Pay de Limon – Lime Flan

1 baked pie crust, 20 cm in diameter
110g (4oz) double cream
110 ml (4 fl oz) condensed milk
4 eggs, separated
225g (8oz) sugar
6 slices lime, halved
225 ml (8 fl oz) fresh lime juice
110 ml (4 fl oz) water
55 ml (2oz) gelatine
pinch of salt

Bring lime juice, sugar and water to the boil and let cool. Stir gelatine and salt into the mixture. Beat egg yolks into mixture. Whisk egg whites and beat in cream and condensed milk. Combine the two mixtures together and pour into the pie shell. Refrigerate for 2 hours, decorate with lime slices and serve.

Pina

The pineapple, ('Ananas sativus'), ananas, or 'pina' in Spanish, is also a native of the Caribbean and grows in the centre of a crown of around 30 long spiky leaves. The pineapple is grown widely in Cuba, and is suited to a hot, almost desert-like climate. The spiny leaves were once fashioned into Spanish ladies' head-dresses, or mantillas. The juice of the luxurious fruit is a well-known meat tenderiser, and the early Cuban Amerindians made a beverage from it. The fruit of the pineapple takes around fifteen months to mature, and is now grown as a lucrative cash crop in Cuba. On his second voyage to the

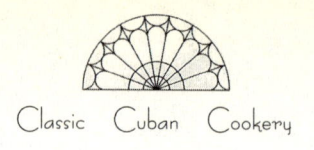

New World, Columbus discovered the delightful pineapple. The story goes that friendly Cuban Amerindians presented Columbus with the fruit as a symbol of hospitality. Since then, throughout Cuban and Caribbean architecture, the pineapple shaped finial has been a common decoration on the entrances to country houses. This practice can also be seen in 18th century European architecture. There are several ways that a pineapple can be used in culinary delights. In Cuba, it is often used as a container for the drink, pina colada, or as a dessert dish with cheese, or as a container for a dessert preparation. Cuba's famous helado, or ice cream, often features pineapple chunks.

Flan de Pina – Pineapple Tart

   450 ml (16 fl oz) fresh pineapple juice
   8 eggs, beaten
   225g (8oz) granulated sugar
   1 tbs gold rum

Grease a large baking dish. Boil pineapple juice and sugar to a syrup and let cool. Stir in the rum, and beat mixture into the eggs. Put baking dish in roasting tray, which is quarter full of water. Pour mixture into baking dish. Bake for about 1 hour in pre-heated oven at 350 degrees. Remove from oven, let cool, then chill.

Preparing Pineapples

To prepare a pineapple, cut an inch slice from the top and bottom with a sharp knife. Stand the fruit up on a board, and cut thick strips of the skin off, downwards, with a sawing motion. Next, turn the skinned pineapple on its side, getting rid of the prickly pieces with a circular cut. Now remove the hard, inedible, central core, and the fruit is

Desserts

ready for serving. Pineapples can also be used as a container for a drink or dessert. Cut the top inch from the head of the fruit, and cut down, between the flesh and the skin, until you have removed a conical-shaped section of the fruit. Dice the fruit cut out, to be used in the dessert or drinks, or slice it to made an appetising Cuban side dish by placing the sections on wedges of cheese.

Piña Sabor – Pineapple Delight

1 pineapple, skinned and cored, and cut into rings
juice of 1 lime
5g (1/4oz) ground coriander
10g (1/2oz) ground nutmeg
5g (1/4oz) ground ginger
5g (1/4oz) ground cinnamon
1 tbs honey
175g (6oz) soft brown sugar
150ml (1/4 pint) water

Grill pineapple rings until soft. Combine all other ingredients in pan and bring to boil. Remove from heat and pour over pineapple rings. Serve with vanilla ice cream.

Piña y Miel – Honey and Pineapple Sorbet

275 ml (10 fl oz) pineapple juice
75 ml (3oz) water
50g (2 oz) honey
10g (1/2oz) gelatine, dissolved in 2 tbs hot water
1 egg white

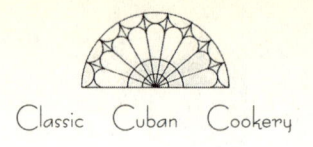

rind of 2 limes
juice of 2 limes
2 tbs caster sugar

Put the juice, honey, lemon rind and sugar in a pan. Bring to the boil whilst stirring and then boil for 4 minutes. Remove from heat and add lemon juice and gelatine. Strain mixture in a freezer tray, cool and freeze for 30 minutes. Beat egg whites until smooth. Freeze the resulting mixture for one hour. Remove mixture from the freezer and whisk until smooth. Return to cold compartment, whisking every hour for 4 hours. Leave in freezer overnight. Serve in chilled glasses, with a spoon that has been dipped in hot water.

Vanilla

Of the more than 17,000 varieties of orchids, vanilla ('Vanilla fragrans') is the only one which produces an exotic perfume from its pod and bean. Originating in Mexico, vanilla, or 'tlilxochitl', was the ancient Aztecs' favourite additive to cocoa, chocolate, or 'xocoatl', which gave their drink a musky flavour, tempered with chilli. The Spanish conquistador, Bernal Diaz, reported that Montezma consumed vast quanities of this beverage. This drink was probably also known to the early Cuban inhabitants, as the vanilla orchid is just one of the 250 orchid varieties endemic to the island.
Over 800 different orchids, including the Vanilla frangrans, can be seen in the orchid gardens of Soroa, in western Cuba. Vanilla, or Vainilla, in Spanish, is the third most expensive spice. The long green pods are harvested before they are ripe. The vanilla orchid can only be pollinated in the wild by one particular variety of bee, and one type of hummingbird, but in 1841 it was found that man could pollinate the orchid by crushing the stamen and pistil together. Until this time, the Spanish had jealously guarded their New World territorial sources of the spice, establishing a monopoly that lasted over 33 years. The pod, or bean, has to be cured to release its pungent odour, by steeping it in

Desserts

boiling water when green, and about seven inches long. The pods are then sweated in cloth, matured, and oven-dried slowly, over several weeks, until the white crystals appear on the pod's now deep brown surface, showing that it is ready to exude its fragrance, said by some to be an aphrodisiac. Vanilla is a traditional flavouring of this classic Cuban dessert.

CARAMELITO DE VAINILLA – VANILLA CARAMEL

    200g (7oz) castor sugar
    4 egg yolks
    1 egg
    50g (2oz) vanilla pods
    275 ml (1/2 pint) double cream
    55 ml (2 fl oz) water

Boil half the sugar and water into a caramel, set aside. Whisk half the sugar, eggs and egg yolks into thick paste. Boil cream and vanilla together in pan. When boiling, add to egg mixture, stirring vigorously. Let cool. Grease four caramel dishes, and pour a little caramel into each. Fill dishes with cream mix until 3/4 full. Place dishes in cooking dish half full of water. Cook in 150ºC (300ºF) degree oven until golden brown on top.
Cool and turn upside down to serve.

CHURROS – SPICY CUBAN BUNS

    1 vanilla pod
    1 tbs anise seed
    3 tbs sugar

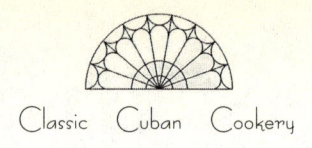

275ml (1/2 pint) vegetable oil for frying
350g (12oz) bread rolls, uncooked

Put vanilla pod, sugar and anise seed in jar. Seal and shake. Leave sugar for at least a day, for vanilla to flavour sugar. Heat a large saucepan with cooking oil, until very hot. Tear rolls into small, plum-size pieces. Drop the pieces with tongs into hot oil. Cook until golden. Drain on kitchen paper. Remove vanilla pod from sugar. Pour sugar into paper bag. Put churros into bag. Seal and shake, to dust churros.

PUDIN DE ARROZ - CUBAN RICE PUDDING

750ml milk
2 egg yolks, beaten
500 ml cooked round rice
125ml sugar
1 tsp brown sugar
1 tbs Cuban honey
1 tsp vanilla essence
1 tsp allspice
1/2 tsp cinnamon
2 tsp Gold rum
2 tbs breadcrumbs
pinch of salt
2 tbs melted butter
250ml raisins, soaked for 1 hour
125ml cubed pineapple

Combine milk, salt, sugars and honey, in pan. Add rice, vanilla and allspice, bringing slowly to boil. Stir, and simmer gently for 10 minutes. Add raisins and rum. Stir and remove from heat. Grease large baking dish. Pour melted butter into dish. Sprinkle with breadcrumbs. Pour mix into the dish. Top with pineapple chunks. Sprinkle with cinnamon. Bake in pre-heated oven for 30 minutes at 360 degrees. Serve when top is browned.

Zapote

The Zapote, ('Manilkara zapota'), sapodilla, or nispero, is a velvety-skinned, brown, oval fruit with a sweet, grainy flesh around small, inedible, shiny black seeds, centrally arranged in a star-shape. This is considered to be the Caribbean's most delightful fruit. Zapote is a good source of vitamin A, and it also contains some calcium. An excellent jam can be made from the bright orange-coloured fruit, which can also be eaten raw. Zapote can also be stewed, and tastes a bit like apricot and brown sugar. The flesh is often used as a filler for cakes, and the subtlety of the zapote's flavour can be brought out with the addition of lime juice. A similar fruit, the Mammee Colorado, ('Mammea americana'), grows on a tree which can reach 70 foot in height, and it resembles a rusty cannonball in shape and size. This sweet pulpy fruit can be used in a number of desserts and to flavour ice creams. Other varieties of the Zapote include the Sapodilla ('Achras sapota'), the Sapote ('Calocapum mamosum'), and the Green sapote ('Calocorum viride'). These fruit contain 94 calories per 100 grams.

ZAPOTE SORBET

    4 zapote, peeled, seeded and chopped in pieces
    2 packs of gelatine
    8 tbs syrup

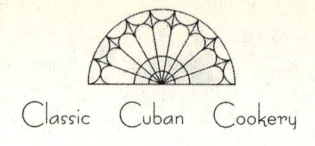

juice of two limes
1/2 tsp salt
225 ml (8 fl oz) water

Blend Zapote chunks in blender until smooth. Dissolve gelatine in water. Whisk syrup, lime juice, and salt, into gelatine mix. Slowly whisk the Zapote blend into mixture. Pour into baking dish, and cover with foil. Freeze for 3 hours, stirring occasionally. Return mixture to blender and blend until fluffy. Freeze again for 2 hours, until firm.

TORTITA MAMMEY – MAMMEY PANCAKE

4 fresh ripe mammeys
2 eggs
5 tbs flour
1 tbs sugar
275 ml (10 fl oz) milk
6 tbs sunflower oil

Place flour in a bowl and make a well. Break eggs into the well. Add the sugar and then the milk gradually, beating all the time. Beat the batter until it is smooth. Leave batter to rest for 15 minutes. Peel and seed the mammeys. Purée the flesh and stir it into the batter. Put the mixture into the freezer for 30 minutes. Heat 1 tbs oil in a pan and place 1 tbs of the mixture into a pan and fry lightly for 2 minutes on each side. Make about 12 tortitas with the mixture and the oil. Serve with syrup or guava paste.

Classic Cuban Cookery

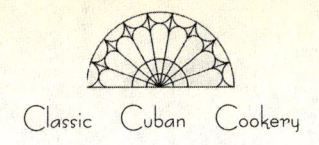

Coffees

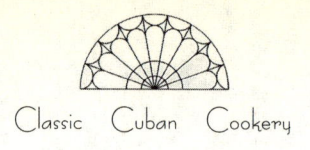

The Nacional Hotel, Havana

The Nacional Hotel, Havana is one of Cuba's most elegant and prestigious hotels. In 1933, the entire government and the military barricaded themselves into the Nacional, during a general strike against Batista's dictatorship. This hotel was a favourite of Frank Sinatra and in 1946, Meyer Lansky and 'Lucky' Luciano threw a birthday party for 'Ole Blue Eyes' in the hotel. Apart from being the centre of Mafia activities in Havana, the Nacional was also a favoured holiday residence for many luminaries of stage and screen. Marlon Brando stayed here, as did Winston Churchill. Graham Greene's character, Wormold, in 'Our Man in Havana', played out his final act in the restaurant of the Nacional. The Nacional's La Arboleda restaurant is considered the most ornate and prestigious in Havana. The hotel has a swimming pool and a nightclub, the 'Caberet Parisien'.

Coffees

Coffee in Cuba

Coffee is Cuba's third most important agricultural crop, and the country's fifth major export, and it is the world's most popular beverage. Coffee can only grow between the tropics of Cancer and Capricorn and Cuba just lies within these latitudes. Coffee grows as a fruit, which is known as a cherry, on a 4 metre high, evergreen bush ('Coffea arabica'). When ripe, the coffee cherries are hand picked although sometimes the cherries are left until they are ripe enough to be shaken from the tree. The cherry surrounds two coffee seeds or beans, which are separated and sun-dried. When opened, the beans are greenish, but become dark brown when dried and roasted to release their characteristic aroma. One tree can produce 2-4 kilos of coffee cherries.

Cuba produces many varieties of coffee, although the Arabica variety is most common. The dark aromatic bean is finely ground, and around a tablespoon of grounds will make one large cup of coffee. The most commonly used method of preparation is by bringing the grounds and water to the boil in a jug, and letting the froth subside before pouring.

In Cuba, coffee is generally served very hot with lots of sugar in a small cup, accompanied by a glass of cool water. The traditional clay, Cuban coffee cup has no handle, is thimble shaped and has a small rim around the top. Even the handled cups used in cafés and restaurants are smaller than demi-tasse. Many Cuban coffee recipes include the addition of rum.

Cuban mesclado is a coffee and chicory blend, whereas Café Americano is the closest equivalent to the instant coffee served in Europe. 'Carrajino' is favoured by most Cubans, and is a very strong coffee laced with white rum. In Santiago de Cuba, the La Isabelica Coffee Shop, serves a wide variety of coffees. Rum, gin, vermouth, liqueurs, orange, lemon and vanilla are some of the ingredients in La Isabelica's repertoire, and Caffea arrabiga is its name for the local brew, with Rocio de Gallo being the house speciality. Coffee is also an ingredient in Cuban candies, cakes, jellies and ices, and in the coffee liqueur produced in the distilleries. Cubita is the national coffee ministry and packages of Cuban coffee beans and ground coffee is sold to visitors as souvenirs.

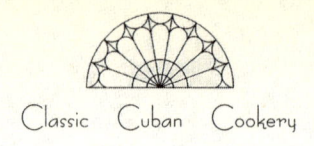

Copa de la Amistad

    45ml espresso
    30ml Aguadiente (raw sugar spirit)
    30ml extra aged rum
    2 tsp sugar
    slice of orange and slice of lime

Prepare the espresso coffee. Pour the aguadiente and rum into a champagne glass. Dissolve the sugar in the rum. Stir in the coffee and garnish with orange and lime.

Coffee was first introduced to the Caribbean by the French Captain, Gabriel de Clieu in the 1710s when he bought a sapling to Martinique from King Louis XIV's greenhouse. By 1728 the first coffee crop was harvested in Jamaica, and it was introduced to Cuba in 1748. Its importance grew when 27,000 French sugar and coffee planters migrated from neighbouring Haiti and built 51 'cafetales' or coffee plantations in the Sierra Maestre mountains near Santiago de Cuba. During the Ten Years War (1868-1878) the revolutionary forces demanded the destruction of the coffee plantations which employed slave labour. However, one of these cafetales has been preserved and is now a museum.

Cafe Fariseo

    30ml hot coffee
    25g grated chocolate
    30ml Carta Blanca rum
    25g sugar
    whipped cream

Coffees

Pour rum, chocolate and sugar into a coffee cup. Stir the mixture and add coffee. Decorate with whipped cream

> Six years after the arrival of the French coffee planters in 1797, free trade in Cuba was made legal and the farmers and planters began growing cocoa, sugar and tobacco in earnest. Most of the exiled planters remained in the region around Santiago de Cuba in the south, which is near Haiti. The French had ruled Haiti until the revolution, when the plantation slaves went on the rampage in a dreadful slaughtering spree. The slaves mostly originated from the Congo region in and those arriving in Cuba with the French exiles brought their culture, traditions, and recipes with them, including variations on coffee preparation.

Cloves

Until the end of the 18th century, the Dutch held a monopoly on cloves. The French began propagating the 40 foot high evergreen trees, of which cloves are the dried unopened buds on their colonies of Mauritius and Cayenne in South America. The name for this spice comes from the latin for nail - 'clavus' - as the buds resemble a nail, and the Spanish know the buds as 'clavo', which is also the word for nail. Cloves are used in a multitude of culinary recipes and they contain a powerful, volatile and antiseptic oil. Cloves are also an ingredient in perfumes and soaps, and the oil is used against toothache, to aid digestion and relieve diarrhoea. The clove buds are sometimes ground and the leaves and stalks are used in the preparation of vanillin or artificial vanilla.

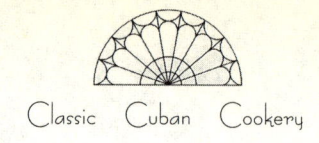

Cafe Fuego

    16g espresso coffee
    60ml Anejo rum
    2 cloves
    1 cinnamon stick
    15g sugar
    rind peel of a lime and orange
    whipped cream

Put rum, cloves, cinnamon and peels in a ladle. Add sugar and warm over a flame. Strain into two cognac glasses, pour in hot coffee and serve with whipped cream decoration.

Cafe Mazzagran

    45ml strong espresso coffee
    30ml Maraschino
    12g sugar
    1 cube of ice
    stick of sugar cane

Place ice in coffee. Add coffee, maraschino and sugar. Stir well. Serve with a stick of sugar cane pith.

Coffee is normally made by machine, but there are still a few places that use the traditional infusion method, which takes a little longer. You will find this method used in the campo, or countryside and in rustic resorts. Often, after sugar has been added to the tiny cup of coffee, a small section of pith is cut from a stalk of sugar cane, and used to stir the coffee with, and to chew on. Cuba exports coffee and sugar, but a fair percentage of output is consumed locally. In resort areas, the visitor's demand for instant coffee has grown and now café Americano is served in most hotels. There are several cafés in Cuba devoted to the production of Cubita coffee, the national label. In the Plaza de Armas in Old Havana, there is the Casa de Café, a replica of the city's once bustling coffee houses, and this serves the real café cubano.

Cafe a la Llama

45ml espresso coffee
30ml Carta Blanca rum
10g sugar

In a large coffee cup, mix hot coffee and sugar. Flambe rum in a glass and pour into coffee.

Cafe Jengibre

10g freshly ground coffee
1/4 tsp freshly grated ginger
10g honey
single cream
45ml water

Mix the ground coffee and ginger together. Filter with boiling water. Pour the honey into the cup and stir in the coffee. Pour in the single cream.

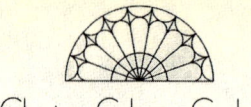

Classic Cuban Cookery

Classic Cuban Cookery

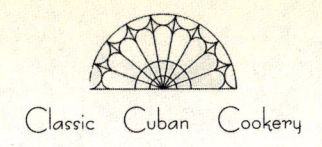

Cocktails

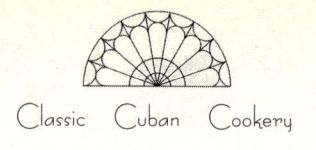

Tropicana Restaurant - Havana

La Tropicana Nightclub was built on the old Villa Mina farm just outside Havana, and opened in December 1931, billed as the 'biggest nightclub in the world'. It became an open-air nightclub in 1939 and now more than 200 dancers, as well as bands and Afro-Cuban ensembles present one of the most flamboyant shows in the world. This 'Paradise Under the Stars' has hosted some of the most famous names in music and dance, including Carmen Miranda, Rita Montander, Nat King Cole and Benny More. The club is set in over 3 hectares and is landscaped with royal and coconut palms, mango and genip trees. At the entrance is a magnificent fountain created by Rita Longo, the celebrated Cuban sculptress. The Tropicana seats an audience of 1,050 around a revolving stage, although the show is held throughout the central arena, bar and restaurant. Enthralled visitors can see a sequence of shows and tableaux depictng various Cuban historical and social events, depicted in dance and accompanied by a range of music from classical to salsa. The extravaganzas are performed by Cuba's leading dancers, mostly from the Cuban Ballet School, one of the world's leading ballet troupes, and are dressed in the most exotic costumes imaginable. The 450-seat Crystal Arches hall, where shows are held should a short tropical downpour be imminent, has a huge bar, facilities in the Panoramic Restaurant to seat 160 diners, and has its own dance floor. Productions at the Tropicana nightclub last for around an hour and a half, and meals and bottles of rum can be served at tables in the auditorium. The Tropicana Club is not lightly called 'A Paradise Under The Stars'.

Cocktails

The Story of Cuban Rum

Rum is an essential ingredient in the Cuban kitchen and is commonly used in recipes, coffees, in cocktails, as well as being enjoyed neat.
Sugar Cane ('Saccharum officinarum') is a type of grass which was originally imported from the Canary Islands to Cuba, but it is indigenous to India. Molasses, which is the basis of alcohol and rum production was being exported from Cuba long before a proper rum was distilled there. It is thought that rum got its name from the ending of the Latin sugar cane, although in Spanish, rum is known as ron.
The first detailed account of rum production was drafted in 1667, although raw rum, had been produced for at least a century before that. In 1714, King Phillip of Spain prohibited the production of rum in Cuba, and so the process was driven underground until the English took Havana in 1762.
At this time, rum was described as a 'strong brandy' and when free trade became legal in 1797, it became an important export. The first rum bar in Havana opened in 1819 - it is still open and is known as El Floridita.
By 1825 there was such a severe glut of molasses that the excess would flow into the drains - that was until more distilleries were built, and by the 1830s, Cuba built its steam engine railway - the first to be built in the Americas - to transport the molasses around the island. During the 1830s, the major market for Cuban rum, which was still an unrefined product, was the US. Once exported, the Americans would mix the rum with more molasses to make it more palatable. By 1848, modern distilleries were being built across the island, and the oldest still surviving is the 1873 factory at Santa Cruz del Norte, east of Havana. New types of rum were being created with the advent of modern techniques, and in the early 1860s, the Real Junto de Fomento in Havana offered a prize to the factory producing the best rum, which was won by Don Facundo Bacardi in 1862. The contest also led to the improvement and development of many brands, including Havana Club, which is now Cuba's leading rum.

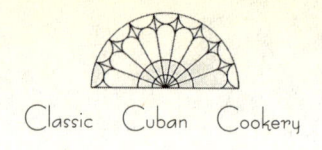

The Mafia Connection

During the US prohibition, which began in 1919, Meyer Lansky joined a gang organised by Arnold Rothstein, with the plan to smuggle Scotch whisky from Europe to the US via Cuba and the Bahamas. This was shipped from Cuba using fast speedboats that would wait outside the 3 mile limit on the US East coast, which would dodge the customs and gunboats. One famous brand of whisky was 'King's Ransom', which was bottled at Al Capone's rum distillery on Cuba's north coast. Capone would also ship his rum into dry America using this route.

When prohibition was due to be repealed in 1933, Langsky and others got together to put in a quarter of a million dollars each to set up a gambling racket in Cuba, to replace the soon-to-be-lost alcohol smuggling racket. Casinos, narcotics and prostitution were where the gangsters' fortunes lay in Cuba but Lansky continued to sell bootleg liquor, untaxed through his Molanska Corporation. Gambling soon overtook his smuggling, as he opened the biggest casino in Havana in the Hotel Nacional and leased the national Cuban racetrack. Al Capone's factory closed, but it still stands to this day.

The Bacardi Story

'Fifteen Men on a dead man's chest,
Yo-ho-ho, and a bottle of rum!
Drink and the devil had done for the rest -
Yo-ho ho, and a bottle of rum!'
Robert Louis Stevenson, Treasure Island

Around the time that Stevenson was born, a Spanish immigrant from Catalonia, Don Facundo Bacardi y Maso settled in Santiago de Cuba, the island's second city. He

Cocktails

established a small wine shop, to sell cheap Spanish wines to other immigrants, but in the back of his shop he had a home-made rum still, producing illegal spirit for his family and friends. Many Cubans made this local drink in their homes, known as 'aguardiente', or 'burning water'. It was a near pure alcohol, distilled from sugar and then watered down. The authorities were aware that Cuba's rum was inferior compared to those produced in the British West Indies, and so offered a cash prize to anyone who could formulate a fine, smooth light rum.

Bacardi set to work with an Englishman named John Nunes, experimenting over several months. They eventually came up with the winning formula, an exquisite golden rum. Nunes decided to leave Cuba with his share of prize money, but Bacardi was determined to capitalise on their discovery, searching for premises where he could mass-produce his celebrated drink. Against advice, Bacardi bought a run-down warehouse in the outskirts of Santiago de Cuba. Not only had it been abandoned for years, but it was infested with vampire bats.

Bacardi left the colony of blood-sucking bats in the beams, but he found it hard to find employees who were prepared to work under the gaze of the bats. He decided to make a feature of it, using the bat as his logo for Bacardi Rum. However, the bats, who had become his symbol fled one night en masse, probably intoxicated by the fumes.

Within a few years, Cuban rum became internationally acclaimed as the finest rum in the world. At the international drinks festival held in Matanzas, Cuba in 1881, Bacardi won the gold medal, and went on to win it every year until 1900.

In October 1960, the new revolutionary government of Cuba nationalised the entire rum production of the island, but by that time the Bacardi factory had fled to Puerto Rico, together with their precious recipe. Today, not a drop of Bacardi rum is produced in its birthplace, but factories in Nassau, the Bahamas, Puerto Rico, Canada, Spain and Mexico produce millions of gallons of Bacardi annually. However, the wily Cuban distillers had not forgotten the magical Bacardi recipes and Bacardi is made in Cuba today, bottled under a different label since a law suit prevented its marketing under the famous bat logo.

Classic Cuban Cookery

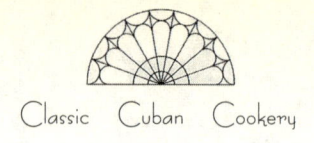

The Cocktail

The derivation of the word cocktail is almost lost in the mists of time, but it is known that the first reference to a mixed rum drink goes back to the days of Sir Francis Drake (1540-96). There was a Mexican tree known as 'Cola de Gallo' or 'Cock's Tail'. Pirates would infuse the roots of this tree in illegal, raw rum. Another possible derivative of the word cocktail comes from the French inhabitants of New Orleans, who imbibed a mixed rum drink known as 'coquetier', which was shortened to 'cocktay' and they would stir the drink with a tail feather of a fighting cockerel. Another explanation is that from the effects of the drink, one's tail perks up, rather like that of the cockerel.

There are probably thousands of ideas as to the origin of the word cocktail, many no doubt exaggerated by over-imbibing the subject matter itself!

There are about 250 rum-based cocktails, made from the hundreds of varieties of rum from the Caribbean. Colour does not necessarily denote the strength of a rum, but most of Cuba's rums are not very dark and not very strong. They are, however excellent for creating a variety of cocktails. Probably the most famous Cuban cocktail is the frozen Daiquiri. Stories vary as to the origins of the Daiquiri, but it is most likely that the American mining engineer Jennings Cox invented it when he was working in a small town of the same name in 1896.

There are 4 different recipes for the Daiquiri.

Cocktails

Daiquiri 1

    2 fl oz light dry rum
    1 tsp sugar
    juice of half a lime
    6 crushed ice cubes

Daiquiri 2

    2 fl oz light dry rum
    1 tsp sugar
    1 tsp grapefruit juice
    1 tsp Maraschino
    juice of half a lime
    6 crushed ice cubes

Daiquiri 3

    2 fl oz old gold rum
    1 tsp sugar
    1 tsp Maraschino
    juice of half a lime
    6 crushed ice cubes

Classic Cuban Cookery

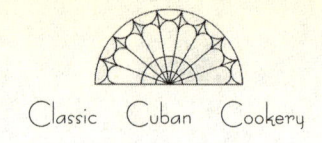

Pink Daiquiri

    2 fl oz light dry rum
    1 tsp sugar
    1 tsp Grenadine
    1 tsp Maraschino
    juice of half a lime
    6 crushed ice cubes

Combine ingredients in a cocktail shaker. Shake vigorously. Wipe the rim of a champagne glass with lime, and dip in some sugar. Pour mixture into the glass. Serve with two short straws.

> By 1898, two years after the beginning of the Second War of Cuban Independence, the United States' commercial interests in Cuba were being jeopardised by skirmishes between the Spanish troops and Cuban rebels. The Spanish fleet had been blockaded in Santiago de Cuba bay, when the US took the island. President McKinley landed 6,000 troops on Daiquiri Beach, including an officer named Teddy Roosevelt.
> The American troops quickly overcame the Spanish, and celebrated with Cuban rum, mixed with a new American beverage, Cola. They called the drink 'Cuba Libre', or 'Free Cuba', Quixotically named by American marines!

Cuba Libre

    2 oz of light dry rum
    juice of half a lime
    peel slice from lime

4 ice cubes
Cola to taste

Combine rum and ice in glass. Pour lime juice over ingredients. Add slice of lime peel, and pour in cola to taste. Stir well.

The Mojito

Ernest Hemingway first visited Cuba, in 1928, when he was 29 years old. Four years later, he returned, and spent 2 months at the Ambos Mundos Hotel in Old Havana. From 1932 to 1940, Hemingway lived in Room 511, writing the drafts of 'For Whom the Bell Tolls', and 'To Have and Have Not'. He was to spend a total of 22 years in Cuba. In 1940, the writer bought a large farmhouse, La Vigía, just outside Havana, and became a frequent visitor to the El Floridita bar, where his bartender friends, Constantino Ribailagua, and Eugenio Rob Iedo, would mix his favourite Daiquiri, a 'Papa Doble', made without sugar. From the Floridita, Papa 'Hemingway' would go to eat at the restaurant, La Bodeguita del Medio, where he would drink another famous Cuban tipple, the Mojito.

Hierbabuena

Hierbabuena, which means 'good grass' is a variety of mint that has been cultivated in Cuba since at least 1535. It is used medicinally and in recipes and is familiar as the plant ingredient in the mojito cocktail.

Mojito

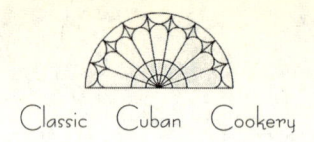

    2 fl oz light dry rum
    1/2 tsp sugar
    juice of half a lime
    sprig of Hierbabuena mint (normal mint will do)
    2 ice cubes
    soda

Combine sugar and lime juice in a highball glass. Add Hierbabuena sprig, crushing in hard into the mixture. Add ice and rum. Top up with soda, and stir well.

The pineapple is practically a symbol of Cuban hospitality. For centuries, ever since Columbus found it growing on the island, the pineapple has been used as a welcome sign in architectural decoration, especially on gateposts. The top is sometimes cut off the fruit, and the centre scooped out, to form a cup for another of Cuba's famous cocktails. Pina Colada means 'strained pineapple' in Spanish.

Pina Colada

    2 fl oz light dry rum
    1 fl oz coconut cream
    1 fl oz lime juice
    2 fl oz pineapple juice
    4 crushed ice cubes
    1/2 tsp vanilla essence (optional)

Blend all ingredients together in a blender. Pour into glass, or pineapple cup. Serve with straw and cherry.

The coconut is the source of many cooking ingredients. The coconut, the fruit of a palm growing across Cuba, but particularly along the shoreline, is the source of many cooking ingredients, such as dessicated, or shredded, coconut meat, coconut milk, and coconut butter.
The dried kernel, which is a nut in the centre of a large, green husk, is the source of coconut oil. When picked fresh, the top of the husk and nut can be removed to form a cup, ideal for filling with a local Cuban delicacy, Saoco.

SAOCO

> 2 fl oz light dry rum
> 4 fl oz coconut milk from the fresh coconut
> 4 ice cubes

Combine ingredients in freshly topped coconut, or glass. Stir well, and serve with two long straws.

There are a number of internationally-known cocktails which are not only Cuban in origin, but have a Cuban name.

CUBANITO

> 2 fl oz light dry rum
> 1/4 fl oz lime juice

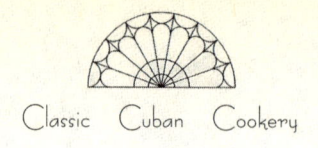

    1 tsp Worcestershire sauce
    tomato juice
    pinch of salt and pepper
    2 ice cubes

Add ingredients to ice cubes in a highball glass. Top up with tomato juice, and stir well.

Cuba Linda

    1 fl oz French dry vermouth
    1 fl oz light dry rum

Chill, don't shake and strain into cocktail glass. Garnish with olive and lemon peel.

Cuba Bella

    1 fl oz light dry rum
    1/2 fl oz extra aged dry rum
    1 tsp lime juice
    1/2 fl oz Creme de Menthe
    cracked ice
    slice of orange
    sprig of hierbabuena mint

In a shaker, mix the rum with the lime. Pour Creme de Menthe over ice in a glass. Add light rum and lime. Pour in aged rum. Serve garnished with orange slice and mint sprig.

Cocktails

A number of famous barmen served both luminaries and gangsters in the bars of Havana from the 1920's to the late 1950's. From the Duke and Duchess of Windsor, Jean Paul Sartre, Francoise Sagan, Graham Greene, and Tennessee Williams, to Errol Flynn, Lou Costello, Spencer Tracy, Douglas Fairbanks, Ava Gardner, Gloria Swanson, Brigitte Bardot, and Jimmy Durante, Havana's bars were a magnate for stars and personalities. The celebrated singers, Caruso, Nat King Cole, Eartha Kitt, and Carmen Miranda, frequented the bars of Havana's plush hotels, and Ava Gardner, Mary Pickford, Greta Garbo, Lillian Gish, and Douglas Fairbanks, all had Cuban cocktails named after them, as did the pirate, Henry Morgan. Apart from the latter, many of the rich and famous of the era were served by Havana's best barmen, like Maragato, at the old Florida Hotel, and Manteca, of the Pasaje Bar. Celestino Gonzalez probably provided the drinks for Frank Sinatra at the Tropicana Nightclub in 1946. One of the most famous of Old Havana's bars, was Sloppy Joe's, opened by Joe Russell in the 1920's, and noted for its Cuban Planter's Punch.

SLOPPY JOE'S PLANTER'S PUNCH

3 fl oz old gold rum
2 fl oz honey
dash of Angostura bitters
1 fl oz lime juice
1/4 tsp grated nutmeg
slice of lime
3 ice cubes

Pour rum, honey, lime juice over ice in tall glass. Add Angostura and grated nutmeg. Stir thoroughly. Serve with slice of lime and long straw.

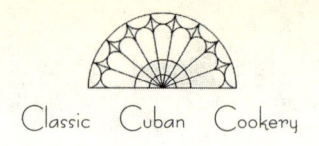

During the 1940's, barmen Chavez and Ricardo, served 'Bugsy' Siegel, 'Lucky' Luciano, and Al Capone at the Club 21, and Antonio Averhoff tended to Ginger Rogers' and Meyer Lansky's barside requirements at the Hotel Riviera. Barman Harold served George Raft at the Monseignor Club, and munitions magnate Du Pont, was served by Armando Aguair at the bar of the 1830 restaurant. It was in the 1940's that barman Jose Maria Vazquez invented another Cuban delight, the Mulata cocktail.

MULATA

1/2 fl oz extra aged rum
3/4 fl oz Creme de Cacao
juice of half a lime
1 tsp shaved chocolate
2 ice cubes crushed

Blend the ingredients in a mixer, except chocolate. Serve in Champagne glass, decorated with sprinkled chocolate.

The writer, Graham Greene, made several visits to Cuba before the Revolution, the setting for his novel 'Our Man in Havana'. After the book's 1958 success, a Graham Special was created in honour of the author.

GRAHAM SPECIAL

1 fl oz Italian vermouth
1 fl oz light dry rum
1/2 tsp sugar

Cocktails

>   juice of half a lime
>   cracked ice
>   slice of pineapple and a cherry

Shake all ingredients, except ice, pineapple and cherries. Strain over cracked ice in a tall glass. Serve with garnishes.

> Havana's cocktail barman of the 1940's and '50's, often invented cocktails named after the hotels in which they worked. Don Enrico, of the Sevilla Biltmore Bar, is credited with the invention of the Sevilla cocktail, probably sipped by guests Enrico Caruso, Gloria Swanson, and Josephine Baker. In 1959, bartender Luis Felipe would have served the new leaders of the Revolution, with his Havana Libre, in the former Havana Hilton Bar. Both Winston Churchill and Marlon Brando would probably have enjoyed the Nacional cocktail at Havana's National Hotel bar.

Sevilla

>   1 1/2 oz of light dry rum
>   1/2 tsp Grenadine
>   1/2 tsp lime juice
>   1/4 tsp sugar syrup
>   3 dashes of Angastura bitters
>   slice of lime
>   cracked ice

Shake ingredients, except lime slice, in a mixer. Strain into 8 ounce glass over cracked ice. Garnish with lime.

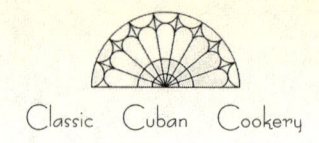

Havana Libre

    1/2 fl oz gold rum
    1 1/2 fl oz extra aged rum
    1 tsp Grenadine
    5 drops of lime juice
    slice of lime
    sprig of mint
    3 ice cubes

In an old fashioned glass, add Grenadine, lime juice and rum. Drop in ice cubes. Garnish with lime slice and mint.

Nacional

    1 fl oz Gold rum
    1/2 fl oz apricot brandy
    1/2 fl oz pineapple juice
    1/4 tsp lime juice
    cracked ice.

Shake all ingredients in a mixer. Serve strained, over cracked ice, into a cocktail glass.

Havana Comodoro

    1 1/2 fl oz extra aged rum

Cocktails

    1/2 fl oz pineapple juice
    dash of Maraschino
    dash of Curacao
    2 ice cubes

Shake all ingredients well. Strain into a cocktail glass. Garnish with a cherry.

Baracoa Special

    1/2 fl oz Santiago White Label rum
    1 tsp coconut cream
    1 tsp grapefruit juice
    2 tsp Marinero dark rum
    2 tsp lime juice

Blend ingredients. Pour over cracked ice in a champagne glass.

Santiago

    1 1/2 fl oz Santiago White Label rum
    1/4 fl oz lime juice
    1/2 fl oz Grenadine
    5 drops Maraschino

Blend ingredients. Pour over cracked ice in a champagne glass.

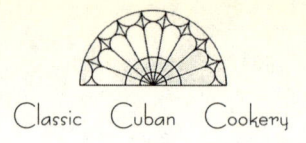

Ostiones

This recipe is for a delicious savoury, which is both a drink and a snack. In many coastal regions around Cuba there are vast stands of mangrove trees, growing with their roots half submerged in salt water. A mussel clings to their roots, which are similar to oysters. This drink calls for half a dozen sweet mussels or oysters in a large glass, one shot of white rum, the juice of half a lime, salt and pepper, a dash of picante sauce, like Tabasco, topped up with tomato juice and downed in one gulp. This is said to be Fidel Castro's favourite aperitif.

SAOCO MARIN COCKTAIL

   2 fl oz light dry rum
   4 fl oz coconut milk from a fresh coconut
   4 ice cubes

Combine ingredients in freshly topped coconut, or glass. Stir well, and serve with two long straws.

Classic Cuban Cookery

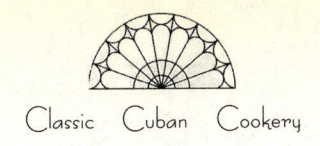

Appendix

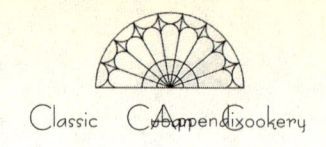

Cuban Restaurants in the UK:

Havana
32 Duke Street
Brighton
Sussex
BN1 1AG
Tel: 01273 773388

Havana
490 Fulham Road
London
SW6 5NH
Tel: 0171 381 5005

Cuba
11 Kensington High Street
London
W8 5NP
Tel: 0171 938 4137

Cuba Libre
72 Upper Street
Islington
London
N1 0NY
Tel: 0171 354 9998

Appendix

Little Havana
1 Leicester Place
London
WC2H 7BP
Tel: 0171 287 0101

Other Cuba Contacts:

Cubana Airlines
49 Conduit Street
London
W1
Tel: 0171 734 1165

Cubanacan (Hotels/Tourism)
Skylines Village
Limeharbour
London
E14
Tel: 0171 537 7909

Cuba Embassy/Tourist Board
167 High Holborn
London
WC1
Tel: 0891 880820

Classic Cuban Cookery

Classic Cuban Cookery

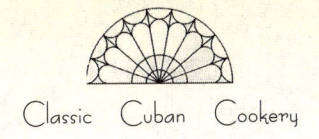

Alternative Ingredients

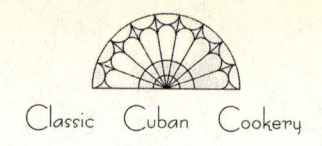

Some of the ingredients in this book may not be widely available. Most can be obtained from large supermarket chains or local West Indian, African, Chinese or Indian markets. In case of difficulty sourcing exact ingredients, the following alternatives may be used.

Fish and Seafood Alternatives

Bass.................................... Mullet, Snapper
Billfish................ Shark, Tuna, Dogfish, Skate
Cod............................... Hake, Haddock
Dogfish.................... Skate, Shark, Tuna
Flounder........ Mullet, Plaice, Sole, Halibut, Snapper
Grouper................ Mullet, Halibut, Snapper
Halibut .... Grouper, Plaice, Sole, Snapper
Herring................................. Mackerel
Plaice.................... Flounder, Sole, Snapper
Pompano .... Snapper, Bass, Flounder
Sprats................................... Sardines
Shark .... Billfish, Dogfish, Skate

Alternative Ingredients

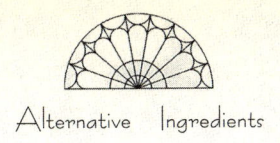

Vegetable and Fruit Ingredients

Arrowroot . . . . Cornflour
Aguadiente . . . . Young white rum
Allspice . . . . Mixed spices
Annatto/Achiote . . . . Oil mixed with saffron or paprika
Sweet potato . . . . Parsnip, Potato
Breadfruit . . . . Jackfruit
Carambola/Starfruit . . . . Kiwi fruit, Grapes
Cassava/Manioc . . . . Yam, Eddoe, Yucca, Taro
Cassava/Manioc flour. Dry, fine-rolled breadcrumbs, Tapioca, Polenta
Chayote . . . . Marrow, Courgette
Eddoe/Taro . . . . Yam, Yucca, Cassava, Potato
Maize . . . . Sweetcorn
Maize cob and husks . . . . Sweetcorn and greaseproof paper
Maize flour . . . . Couscous
Malanga greens . . . . Swiss chard, Spinach
Palm oil . . . . Olive oil and a little paprika
Plantain . . . . Unripe banana
Pomelo . . . . Lychee
Tamarind pulp . . . . Pre-packed tamarind pulp
Tomaton/Tomatillo . . . . Small, green tomatoes or green gooseberries
Yerababuena/Hierbabuena . . . . Mint
Yucca/Jucca/Malanga . . . . Yam, Eddoe, Taro, Potato
Zapote/Mammey/Sapodilla . . . . Unripe pear, Peach

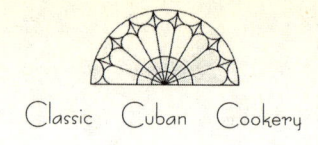

Chilli Alternatives

Fresh Chilli	Heat	Substitute
Anaheim	Medium	New Mexico Red, New Mexico Green
Cayenne	Very hot	Indian chilli
Fresno	Hot	Red or green Jalapeno
Habenero	Hottest	No real substitute
Jalapeno	Hot	Half the Frenso variety
Pimiento	Mild	Poblano, Red bell pepper
Poblano	Mild	Pimiento, half New Mexico Green
Serrano	Hot	Jalapeno, Frenso
Scots Bonnet	Fiery	Tabasco, Cayenne
Tabasco	Very hot	Half the quantity of Habanero

Dried/Smoked Chilli

Chilli	Heat	Substitute
Ancho, Dry Poblano	Medium	Pasilla
Bird's Eye, Piquin	Fiery	Habanero
Cascabel	Medium	Ancho, Pasilla
Cayenne	Very hot	Twice the quantity of Pasilla
Chipotle	Hot	Twice the quantity of Ancho
Guajillo	Mild	Mulato
Habanero	Hottest	Bird's Eye, Piquin
Mulato	Mild	Guajillo
Pasilla	Medium	Ancho, Cascabel

Classic Cuban Cookery

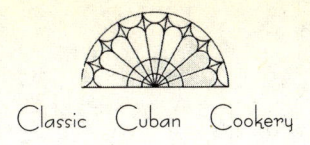

Index

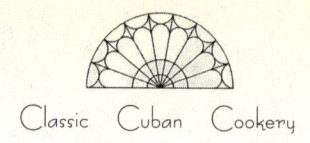

English Index

AUBERGINE BALLS 158
AVOCADO AND TOMATO SALAD 36
AVOCADO SAUCE 99
BAKED MAHI MAHI 132
BANANA BARBECUED POMPANO FISH .130
BANANA BREAD 165
BANANAS AND PORK 73
BARACOA SPECIAL 213
BATABANO BANANA BREAD 162
BASS IN GREEN SAUCE 129
BEEF BURGER FILLERS 27
BLACK BEAN SOUP 52
BLACK BEANS AND CORIANDER 151
CAF A LA LLAMA 195
CAF FARISEO 192
CAF FUEGO 194
CAF JENGIBRE 195
CAF MAZZAGRAN 194
CAMARA'S SWEET POTATO FLAN 152
CASSAVA BREAD 142
CHANGO-STYLE SWEET POTATOES 14
CHERIMOYA ICE 175
CHE-STYLE PUMPKIN WITH PORK 78
CHICKEN AND PUMPKIN STEW 82
CHOCOLATE BANANA BARBARA 168
COCONUT CREAM PIE 171
COCONUT ICE CREAM 172

Index

CRAB WITH PAPAYA	110
CREOLE SHRIMP	113
CREOLE STEW	62
CREOLE-STYLE WRECK FISH	127
CRIOLLO STONE CRABS	112
CUBA BELLA	208
CUBA LIBRE	204
CUBA LINDA	208
CUBAN BANANAS	170
CUBAN BARBECUED PORK	69
CUBAN BEAN FEAST	149
CUBAN BREAD AND BUTTER PUDDING	173
CUBAN CHEESE TOASTIES	26
CUBAN HASH	76
CUBAN HOTPOT	85
CUBAN MEAT AND VEGETABLE PATTIES	28
CUBAN MEAT LOAF	65
CUBAN MEATBALLS IN A HOT SAUCE	81
CUBAN PAPAYA CHEESE	15
CUBAN RICE PUDDING	186
CUBAN ROAST BEEF	67
CUBAN ROLLED BEEF	69
CUBAN SEAFOOD SAUCE	100
CUBAN STUFFED SUCKLING PIG	68
CUBANITO	208
CUBAN-STYLE CONCH SALAD	110
CUBAN-STYLE RED SNAPPER	128
CUCUMBER SALSA	103
DAIQUIRI 1	203

Classic Cuban Cookery

DAIQUIRI 2	203
DAIQUIRI 3	203
DRUNKEN' SAUCE	98
FILLETS OF SWORDFISH	131
FRANCISCAN RED BEAN SOUP	53
FRESH GREEN BEAN SOUP	51
FRICASSE OF BARBECUED CROCODILE	118
GARLIC EDDOES	145
GARLIC MAYONNAISE	154
GARLIC PUREE	155
GINGER AND AVOCADO SOUP	45
GRAHAM SPECIAL	210
GROUND BEEF TAMALE SNACK	23
GUANABANA SOUFFLE	174
GUAVA CRISP	178
GUAVA JELLY	180
HAVANA COMODORO	212
HAVANA LIBRE	212
HAVANA PICKLE SAUCE	96
HONEY AND PINEAPPLE SORBET	183
JACKFRUIT WITH COCONUT MILK	77
LANGOUSTINE EL FLORIDITA	115
LANGOUSTINE	116
LIME FLAN	181
MAIZE AND PEPPER SALAD	37
MAIZE SOUP	49
MAMMEY PANCAKE	188
MANGO CHUTNEY	104
MATANZAS TURTLE FRICASSE	117

Index

MILLIONAIRE'S PALM HEART SALAD 39
MOJITO 206
MOJITO SAUCE AND MARINADE 109
MOORS AND CHRISTIANS (RICE AND BLACK BEANS) 151
MULATA 210
NACIONAL 212
OGUN BEAN FEAST 153
OKRA AND EDDOE SOUP 46
OLD WOMAN'S CLOTHES' (CUBAN STEW) .60
PEANUT BUTTER 98
PEANUT SAUCE 97
PINA COLADA 206
PINEAPPLE DELIGHT 183
PINEAPPLE TART 182
PINK DAIQUIRI 204
PIQUIN CHILLI AND PEANUT SAUCE 97
PIRATE'S PICKLED FISH 125
PLANTAIN SNACK 25
PORK FILLETS CUBAN STYLE 73
PORK RIND SNACKS 17
PRAWN-STUFFED TURNOVERS 114
PUMPKIN AND PORK 79
QUIQUI MARINA'S CALDOSA STEW 71
RAINBOW PEANUT SOUP 48
RANCH STYLE STEAK 75
RED CHILLI SAUCE 102
RICE AND RED BEANS 150
RICE AND SPEARFISH STEAKS 133
RICE STUFFED PEPPERS 80

Classic Cuban Cookery

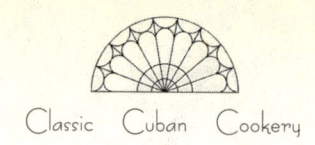

RICE WITH BANANAS 146
ROAST DUCK WITH CHORIZO AND ORANGE STUFFING 84
SALSA HABANERO 105
SANTA ANA-STYLE JUCCA DOUGHNUTS 143
SANTIAGO 213
SAOCO 207
SAOCO MARIN COCKTAIL 214
SEVILLA 211
SHARK MEAT SNACKS 29
SHRIMP TAPAS 15
SLOPPY JOE'S PLANTER'S PUNCH 209
SOFRITO 44
SPANISH-STYLE OMELETTE 158
SPICY CUBAN BUNS 185
SQUID TAPAS 16
STAR-SPANGLED SALAD 177
STUFFED BREADFRUIT 64
SUGAR APPLE SOUFFLE 176
SWEET POTATO TAPAS 16
TAINO TROUT 135
TOASTED PLANTAIN 157
TOMATON SAUCE 101
TUNA WITH RUM SAUCE 126
VAGUERO-STYLE BARBECUED PORK 66
VANILLA CARAMEL 185
VEGETARIAN TAMALES 155
YAM NUGGETS 148
ZAPOTE SORBET 187

228

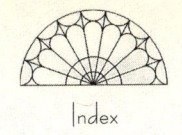

Spanish Index

AGUACATE SALSA 99
ALBONDIGAS BAYAMESE 81
ALIOLI 154
ARAWAK ENSALADA CONCHA 110
ARROZ CON PLATANO 146
ARROZ CUBANO 147
ARROZ Y FRIJOLES COLORADOS 150
ATUN CON RON 126
BACAN BANANA 73
BANANA CUBANA 170
BARACOA SPECIAL 213
BATABANO BANANA BREAD 166
BISTEC EN ROLLO 69
BOLAS DE BERNIENA 158
BONIATILLO CHANGO 14
BONIATO 16
BUNUELOS DE JUCCA COCINADA SANTA ANA 143
CAF A LA LLAMA 195
CAF FARISEO 192
CAF FUEGO 194
CAF JENGIBRE 195
CAF MAZZAGRAN 194
CALABAZA CHE 78
CALABAZA CON CERDO 79
CALAMARES 16
CALDILLO CUBANO 85
CALDOSA QUIQUI MARINA 71

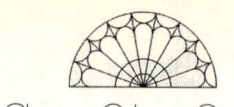

Classic Cuban Cookery

CAMARONES	15
CAMARONES A LA CRIOLLA	113
CARAMELITO DE VAINILLA	185
CARNE ASADA	67
CARNICERO	65
CERDO BARBACOA A LA VAGUERO	66
CHAMPOLA DE CHERIMOYA	175
CHERNA CRIOLLO	127
CHURRASCO LOS RANCHOS	75
CHURROS	185
CICHARRONES	17
COMILONA FRIJOLES	149
COMILONA FRIJOLES OGUN	153
CONGREJO FRUTA BOMA	110
CONGRI SANTIAGO	62
COPA DE LA AMISTAD	192
CRIOLLO STONE CRABS	112
CUBA BELLA	208
CUBA LIBRE	204
CUBA LINDA	208
CUBANITO	208
DAIQUIRI 1	203
DAIQUIRI 2	203
DAIQUIRI 3	203
EMPANADAS	28
ENCHILADA DE CAMARONES	114
ENCHILADOS TIBERON	29
ENSALADA AGUACATE Y TOMATE	36
ENSALADA ELOTE Y PIMIENTO	37

Index

ENSALADA ESTRELLA	177
ENSALATA MILLIONARIO	39
ENSALATA MIXTA A LA CUBANA	34
ESTOFADO CON POLLO Y CALABACITA	82
FILETE DE EMPORADOR REBOZADO	131
FILETES DE CERDO	73
FLAN BATATAS CAMARA	152
FLAN DE PINA	182
FRICASSE DE COCODRILO BARBECUE	118
FRICASSED DE TORTUGA MATANZAS	117
FRIJOLES BAYOS CILANTRO	151
FRUTO DEL PAN DISECADO	64
GRAHAM SPECIAL	210
GUANABANA SOUFFLE	174
GUAVA GELATIMA GUAMA	180
HAVANA ANCHO ADOBO	96
HAVANA COMODORO	212
HAVANA LIBRE	212
HELADO DE COCO	172
JACKFRUIT CON LECHE DE COCO	77
LANGOUSTINE	116
LANGOUSTINE EL FLORIDITA	115
LECHON ASADO	68
MALANGA CON AJO	145
MANTEQUILLA DE MANI	98
MARAQUITA	25
MOJITO	206
MOROS Y CHRISTIONES	151
MULATA	210

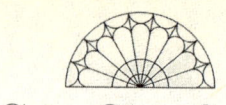

NACIONAL 212
PAELLA CUBANO 119
PAN DE CASABE 142
PAN DE PLATANO 165
PARGO CUBANO 128
PASTEL DE CREMA COCO 171
PASTELES GUAYABA 179
PATO PLATANO 84
PAY DE LIMON 181
PEPINO SALSA 103
PEPITAS DE CUSH CUSH 148
PESCADO EN ESCABECHE 125
PICADILLO PICADURA 76
PICADILLO 'SLOPPY JOE'S' 74
PIMENTIO DISECADO CHORIZO 80
PINA COLADA 206
PINA SABOR 183
PINA Y MIEL 183
PINK DAIQUIRI 204
PIQUIN Y MANI SALSA 97
POMPANO PLATANO 130
PUDIN DE ARROZ 186
PUDIN DIPLOMATICO 173
QUESO FRUTA BOMBA 15
RELLENO DE PICADILLO 27
ROBALO CON SALSA VERDE 129
ROPA VIEJA 60
SALSA BORRACHA 98
SALSA DE CHILLI VERDE 102

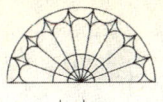

Index

SALSA DE MANI	97
SALSA HABANERO	105
SALSA MARINERO	.00
SANTIAGO	213
SAOCO	207
SAOCO MARIN COCKTAIL	214
SEVILLA	211
SLOPPY JOE'S PLANTER'S PUNCH	209
SOFRITO	44
SOPA DE ELOTE	49
SOPA DE FRIJOLES TIERNOS	51
SOPA DE JENGIBRE Y AGUACATE	45
SOPA DE MANI ARCO	48
SOPA FRIJOLES BAYOSMI CASITA	52
SOPA FRIJOLES FRANCISCO	53
SOPA KIMBOMBO	46
SOUFFLE DE CORAZON	176
TAMALES PICADO	23
TAMALES VEGETARIANO	155
TOMATILLO SALSA	101
TORTILLA ESPANOLA	158
TORTITA MAMMEY	188
TOSTONES CON QUESO	26
TOSTONES DE PLATANO VERDE	157
TRUCHO TAINO	135
ZAPOTE SORBET	187

Books by Andy Gravette

Cuba, An Introduction
Cuba, A Natural History
Official Guide to Cuba
Cuba - Guide
Globetrotter's Guide to Cuba
Map Guide to Cuba
Map Guide to the Canary Islands
The Traveller's Guide - French Antilles
The Traveller's Guide - Netherlands Antilles
Explorer Guide to the Caribbean
Globetrotters' Guide to the Canary Islands
Insight Guide to the Eastern Canary Islands
Insight Guide to the Gambia and Senegal
Landmark Guide to the Gambia
The European Hotel Guide
French Hotel Guide
Visitors Guide to Egypt
Visitors Guide to the Balearic Islands
Windrush - Sardinia
Windrush - Madeira
Suntree Guide to Italy
Architectural Heritage of the Caribbean
Slainte! A Taste of Old Ireland
The Story of Rum in the Caribbean
The Story of the Cuban Cigar
Caribbean Barbecue Cookery